The Balm of Gilead

The Balm of Gilead

WOMEN'S STORIES OF FINDING PEACE

Deseret Book Company
Salt Lake City, Utah

Library of Congress Cataloging-in-Publication Data

The balm of Gilead : women's stories of finding peace.
      p.   cm.
  Includes index.
  ISBN 1-57345-248-3
  1. Mormon women—Biography. 2. Peace of mind—Religious aspects—Mormon Church. 3. Women in the Mormon Church. 4. Mormon Church—Membership. 5. Church of Jesus Christ of Latter-day Saints—Membership. I. Deseret Book Company.
BX8693.B35   1997
289.3'092—dc21   97-5130
[B]   CIP

Printed in the United States of America

10 9 8 7 6 5 4 3 2 1   49510

Contents

v

FINDING PEACE THROUGH PRAYING AND RECEIVING PRIESTHOOD BLESSINGS

FINDING PEACE THROUGH SERVING

FINDING PEACE THROUGH CHANGING PERSPECTIVES AND PRIORITIES

FINDING PEACE THROUGH
ACKNOWLEDGING THE ATONEMENT OF CHRIST

Introduction

_____

The Brigham Young University–Relief Society Women's Conference committee members have recognized that many sisters have a strong desire to participate more fully in the conference. Given the gospel literacy initiative of the Relief Society and desiring to involve more women in the conference, the 1996 Women's Conference committee extended a call for essays through which women could share perspectives on their own life experiences.

The theme for the essay submissions was taken from the address by Relief Society General President Elaine L. Jack entitled "Relief Society: A Balm in Gilead," which was delivered at the general women's meeting in September 1995 (*Ensign,* Nov. 1995, 90–93). The symbolism of the balm of Gilead—a precious emollient and aromatic spice with soothing and healing properties that in biblical times grew prolifically in Gilead, a district east of the River Jordan—seemed particularly appropriate for personal expressions of testimony.

The challenge for women to identify ways of finding peace in their lives also related to the 1994 Primary theme, "The gospel of Jesus Christ can bring me peace," with *peace* defined for the children as "a feeling of love and safety and quiet that comes from the Lord." And there was a connection to Sister Patricia Holland's keynote address to the 1987 Women's Conference, in which she invited sisters to return to "the wholeness of our soul, that unity in our very being that balances the demanding and inevitable diversity of life" ("Many Things . . . One Thing," in A *Heritage of*

Faith, ed. Mary E. Stovall and Carol Cornwall Madsen [Salt Lake City: Deseret Book, 1988], 18).

The invitation to participate struck a responsive chord with the sisters. Essays came and kept coming. Some were painstakingly handwritten by arthritic fingers in a spidery scrawl, others pecked out on an ancient typewriter, still others generated by computer, and some professionally formatted, complete with an e-mail address. All contained the poignant expressions of women eager to share their stories.

The response was overwhelming and heartfelt. The essays kept coming beyond the deadline, and some were even brought to the conference and thrust into the hands of conference committee members. One sister said, "I know it's too late to participate, but I am so grateful for this opportunity to share my life with others." Many expressed appreciation for the invitation to articulate the experiences they had lived as women of faith.

The committee members and reviewers were struck by the wide diversity of women living in a variety of life circumstances who had responded. Essays came from sisters of every description: younger and older; rural and urban; ethnically diverse; sisters of modest means, and others more affluent; women struggling to overcome the effects of childhood abuse and dysfunctional families, and women sheltered in cocoons of lifelong love; sisters functionally illiterate, and others highly educated; women single, and women married; women for whom the gospel is a fresh, new adventure, and others for whom the gospel means a lifetime of dear familiarity; and women for whom pain is a constant companion, women whose sensitivity has been honed by adversity. Their message is profound: there is indeed

a Balm in Gilead,
To make the wounded whole,
There is a Balm in Gilead,
To heal the sin sick soul.

William L. Dawson, in *Recreational Songs* (Salt Lake City:
The Church of Jesus Christ of Latter-day Saints, 1949), 130

2

Their clear message was a testimony of the Savior and the personalness of his love, as expressed in the words to the hymn "Where Can I Turn for Peace?" by Emma Lou Thayne (*Hymns* [Salt Lake City: The Church of Jesus Christ of Latter-day Saints, 1985], no. 129):

> *He answers privately, Reaches my reaching*
> *In my Gethsemane, Savior and Friend.*
> *Gentle the peace he finds for my beseeching*
> *Constant he is and kind, Love without end.*

We begin to know and understand others by the stories we share, for stories connect us as we crisscross our common and our uncommon life experiences. Stories connect us emotionally and spiritually and assure us that others confront similar challenges in their own lives.

This collection chronicles the experiences of sisters who have found peace through obtaining hope and faith, through prayer and priesthood blessings, through serving others, through changing perspectives and priorities, and through acknowledging the blessings of the atonement of Jesus Christ.

These essays are a strong testament of the Savior and may serve as a balm of Gilead for us who read them. May we be lifted and encouraged by the words of our sisters, who were willing to share with us in such heartfelt and personal ways.

Lynn Clark Callister is associate dean of the College of Nursing at Brigham Young University, where her research on the cultural meanings of childbirth has led her to interview many American LDS women, Canadian Orthodox Jewish women, Finnish Lutheran women, Jordanian Muslim women, and Guatemalan Catholic women. She and her husband, Reed Richards Callister, are the parents of eleven children and the grandparents of fourteen. She serves as a stake Relief Society president and as a member of the BYU–Relief Society Women's Conference Committee.

FINDING PEACE
THROUGH OBTAINING
HOPE AND FAITH

Precious Balm

SUSAN CHAMPION SOMMERFELDT

When I was a child, the hymn felt long and slow. While I was still wondering how "air could leave its room this morning," another line of the hymn raised an intriguing question in my curious mind: What happens when the 'Bomb of Gilead' explodes?

Thirty-five years later the question again surfaces, reshaped by life's experiences and a degree of maturity: What *does* happen when the balm of Gilead explodes? What is the balm of Gilead? How have I applied its healing potential? What properties made the ancient balm of Gilead significant enough that its mention survived centuries of scriptural transmission and translation? Why was it so precious?

The Ancient Balm

Various Bible scholars describe a product developed from the sap, bark, or leaves of a tree or bush in the district of Gilead and made into an ointment used as a salve or an oil used as a medicine. The qualities attributed to the salve made it valuable and desirable. Ishmaelite merchants appear to have been carrying the balm when they happened upon Joseph's brothers as they were debating his fate (Genesis 37:25). Ezekiel depicts its merchandising in his time (Ezekiel 27:17). Its distinction as a healing agent is cited in Jeremiah (8:22; 46:11). A pharmacological speculation is that an active ingredient in the compound promoted healing and warded off infection, making the balm both valuable and popular. If the physical properties of the balm were analgesic and antiseptic, we can understand its value. To extend the metaphor, then, how does the spiritual balm address pain and cleanse wounds? Does it also encourage healing and provide protection, enabling me to feel peace?

An Analgesic Balm

As an analgesic or perhaps as a topical anesthetic agent, the early ointment could have relieved pain. Something that removes or diminishes discomfort is always welcome.

When I was six months into my fifth pregnancy, the baby began having serious difficulties. It appeared that labor could begin at any time. My visiting teacher knew I had a doctor's appointment one morning and in the early afternoon phoned to get a report. I conceded that I needed to be careful but tried to sound independent and resourceful. After the call, I wondered how I was going to pull it off this time. I had had difficult pregnancies before, had been ill, had delivered a premature child, and had endured prolonged hospitalizations, but family and friends had rallied in each crisis. This time I felt I had called in all my favors, played all my trump cards, and depleted my cruse of oil. My husband was already carrying a heavy load: he was a new partner in a business and the bishop of our ward, and he was already doing a great deal at home. Making plans and revising strategies failed to relieve my concerns.

The doorbell rang, and in walked my visiting teacher. She had hung up the phone, put on her coat, and walked the mile or so to my house because, she explained, she thought I could use a visit. That was emotional liniment. Sisterhood is a seemingly paradoxical blend of self-reliance and interdependency. With tremendous support from her and numerous others who helped see us through the anxiety, frustration, and logistics, a healthy baby boy eventually joined our family. Balm had been offered and applied with tenderness. I became more aware of the balm of Gilead and gained an insight into how one can compassionately administer it. As I have had opportunity since then to recognize and respond to another's need, I have discovered that the words of former Relief Society General President Barbara Winder are true: "Peace can come to both the giver and receiver as we follow the promptings of the Spirit to serve one another" (*Ensign*, Nov. 1985, 96).

The Antiseptic Balm

The balm of centuries ago could have had antiseptic or antibiotic properties. Microorganisms were unknown at the time, yet the problems caused by infection still existed. It might have seemed like magic for a wound to heal when treated with balm of Gilead when a similar injury without such care could become infected, perhaps even leading to death. Although the process might not have been understood by the one applying the aid, the balm could nevertheless be used with success. An antibiotic characteristic of the mixture would not only treat an infection but prevent one, being protective as well as curative.

The Word of Wisdom is that kind of balm. A *Times and Seasons* editorial teaches: "God only is acquainted with the fountain of action, and the main springs of human events; he knows where disease is seated and what is the cause of it;—he is also acquainted with the spring of health; the balm of Gilead—of life; he knows what course to pursue to restore mankind to their pristine excellency and primitive vigour, and health; and he has appointed the word of wisdom as one of the engines to bring about this thing" (3 [1 June 1842]: 799–800).

So many assertions compete for my consideration in making lifestyle choices. The media misrepresent ideal body types and desirable images; vitamins and other supplements are marketed as crucial to sound health; dangerous dieting ideas and exercise extremes are presented as simple solutions to complex problems. Physical attractiveness seems to have more value than righteousness in our culture. Doctrine and Covenants 89:4 warns us of "evils and designs which do and will exist in the hearts of conspiring men in the last days." Prayerfully pondering the promises and principles revealed in the Word of Wisdom is a protectant, or perhaps an antiseptic, that spares us from damaging demands and gives us specific guidelines. If we follow it, even if we do not fully understand, it protects us from secondary problems.

Protection against the loss of perspective comes from receiving answers to personal prayers. I know that following the prophet brings assurance and peace. Throughout my life I have listened carefully to prophetic counsel. That has required pondering and prayerful study to make decisions that could be ratified through prayer. I completed the first stage of my education before my marriage. I considered carefully subsequent educational or professional opportunities as they arose. A conflict developed on account of the requirement within my profession to maintain a minimum number of clinical hours within a five-year window. Fragments of prophetic teachings swirled in my thoughts each time a decision needed to be made: be prepared to support a family in case of widowhood; mothers should be at home; be articulate as well as affectionate; be a well-educated, well-informed people. Doing the right thing didn't seem as simple as the question of career or family. Over the past twenty years, I have received clear direction I have followed without regret. Prayers have been answered, prophets have been heeded, and faith has allowed the consequences to follow. I suspect I do not understand the extent of how the balm of divine direction has protected me and my family, much as caregivers of old did not understand the pharmacological processes of the healing balm they dispensed. I do, however, understand what the Lord expects of me. The blessings of direction and calmness have been gratefully accepted as I nurture my children and sustain my husband.

The Timeless Balm

Could it be that the balm of Gilead is produced from the yield of the tree of life? The gospel of Jesus Christ protects us from the threat of spiritual death and disease by increasing our knowledge, providing for forgiveness, and allowing opportunity for service. Prayer, study, selfless service, and righteousness compose the balm-producing formula that has been taught by ancient prophets and echoed by those in our own time. Balm has been abundantly available for me as the need has been manifested throughout my life. It has been supplied at times by my own effort, but often it comes through another's compassion. Faith dictates that an ever-ample stock will be accessible as I learn and live the gospel, providing me with pain relief, pureness, and protection. The balm of Gilead which was valuable in the Old Testament world continues to be precious in mine.

Susan Champion Sommerfeldt, a registered nurse, is a homemaker and a student in a post-R.N. baccalaureate program. She and her husband, Don, are the parents of Matt, Rachelle, Mark, Joey, David, James, and Maryn. She serves as a Relief Society visiting teacher and as a member of the activities committee in her ward in Edmonton, Alberta, Canada.

A Daughter of God

WENDY L. VLAZNY

When you're three you work very hard at being "big," but you can't quite shake off being "little." Every day brings a new development, a new skill, or a new word to your ever-increasing vocabulary. With all this growth and change comes the desire for independence and the accompanying frustration of not being "big" enough to achieve it. Often I hear first a screech of frustration, followed by sobs, and then "Mommy, I can't do it," or "Mommy, I'm stuck," or just "Mommy, I need you." Rushing in to save my three-year-old daughter, Kaytlyn, from the latest crisis, I find her in a crumpled heap on the floor, her eyes filled with tears. As she desperately struggles to articulate what she is feeling, I lift her from the floor and extricate her from whatever article of clothing she has bound herself in. Holding her in the rocking chair, stroking her hair as we rock slowly, I softly sing, "I Am a Child of God" until her sobbing has ceased, and the crisis has passed. What comfort she finds in these words. This assurance of her royal heritage and her Father's great love for her brings such peace to this little sister in Zion.

How often I have longed for that same peace. The past four years have been a great struggle for me. I have had to learn to deal with some very debilitating illnesses. The first was the fibromyalgia. After months of excruciating pain and numerous tests—some causing great discomfort—I was incredulous to learn not only that I had this disease but that there is no cure and very little understanding. I was angry. Angry at the doctors for being so inept, and absolutely furious at Heavenly Father for having placed this burden on me. Hadn't I been a dutiful daughter? I had done all that had been asked of me. I had obeyed the commandments, married in the temple, filled my callings, rendered any and all service when asked, and even overpaid my tithing! How, I demanded to know, *how* could this have been done to me? Was my name Job, or what? I felt betrayed.

Month after month, prayer after prayer, I struggled to come to terms with my disease. The drug combination I was originally given made me ill; another was tried with the same effect. Each new road I went down became a dead end: the treatment was either ineffective or made me violently ill. The pain management specialists were scratching their heads. Day after day, I searched the scriptures for acceptance, and day after day I felt I was further and further from my Father. My question was always the same: Why had this cup been handed to me?

Time passed. There were deaths, births, and disappointments. I learned to live with the fibromyalgia, but my prayers, I felt, went unanswered. I was sure Heavenly Father was no longer listening to me. I went through the motions of serving in my callings and doing my visiting teaching, but I avoided attending the temple. I felt unclean, unworthy. I was certain I was being punished for some unrepented offense.

One beautiful, crisp fall morning in 1994 I woke, rose from the bed, and promptly fell to the floor. The pain in my left leg and left arm was horrendous. My leg wouldn't support me. I was unable to walk. The rounds of specialists and testing began again. The diagnosis this time was a slipped disk in my neck. After a few days of bed rest, I was told, I would be up and running again. I was. Two weeks later the disk was out again. It healed, and then it went back out again a week later. Once it popped out while I was working in the Primary nursery, another time while I was giving the Relief Society lesson. Within two months' time all I had to do to put out this disk out was to roll over in my sleep. I lost feeling in my left hand. I would burn myself cooking and not realize that I had done so until I saw the blister forming. I lost weight rapidly, until I weighed barely ninety-five pounds. More tests were ordered. I was losing ground rapidly, and I needed more help than I was getting from the medical professionals.

Christmas 1994 was a sad affair at our house. My parents came from California to try to help make it bright for our young one. I was able to do little. Although Santa came to visit us that year, what I was looking for could not be found in his bag of goodies. The New Year looked as though it would be a repeat of the old.

I was fast approaching the breaking point. I was having difficulty taking care of my toddler child, much less running a household. My business was in ruins, and my world seemed on the brink of collapse. At last, feeling I had not an ounce of strength left, I gave up. Crumpled in a heap on the floor, sobbing, I cried, "Father, I need you." In the blink of an eye, I felt his Spirit reach down and lift me, lovingly reminding me that I am his beloved child, a child of royal heritage. In that instant, I began to accept my situation and find peace. I had spent so much time trying to be "big" when all I needed to do was to be "little." I had learned something about becoming as a little child.

The now-crumbled disk in my neck was removed, and I spent several weeks in bed, recovering. It was a time spent in contemplation of Heavenly Father's great and marvelous works. As in times past, many sisters from the ward rendered overwhelming, loving service. Friends and family members took turns caring for my home and family until I was well enough to do so. I am grateful for a Heavenly Father who loves me, for a Savior who accepted the bitter cup and unselfishly gave his life that I, too, might live, and for an eternal companion who has always honored his priesthood and his family. I have been immensely blessed by my daughter, Kaytlyn, who, when I am feeling at my lowest, will lie down beside me, stroke my hair, and softly sing "I Am a Child of God." And together, as sisters in Zion, we find peace in being his children.

Wendy L. Vlazny is a homemaker and an accountant. She and her husband, Donald, are the parents of two children. She has been a teacher in Relief Society and Primary and a temple district ordinance worker and now serves as her ward newsletter editor.

The Burning Light of Hope

HEATHER HIPPEN

Not long ago I was asked to travel to Santa Cruz, California, to take part in a management training seminar for my company. The days were filled with lectures and work, and the evenings included wonderful dinners and much revelry by both participants and leaders of the seminar. Toward the end of the week there was a celebration dinner and program. I sat sipping my water and watching the crowd become more and more rowdy as alcohol was served more frequently. I began to feel particularly out of place. In fact, I felt as invisible and lost as if I were in a completely foreign country. I excused myself early and walked back to my hotel room.

It had been an honor to be asked to attend this seminar because I was the youngest employee in my department by at least ten years. I had graduated from Brigham Young University less than a year earlier with my master's degree. (Contrary to popular rumor, there is no tuition reimbursement for graduating from BYU twice while remaining single!) Before leaving BYU I had been offered a great job with a well-known corporation and had been promoted to management within six months. I was working my way up the career ladder and enjoying the success and freedom that was mine.

The heavens seemed so quiet and still that night as I left the noise of the party behind me. I walked slowly. No one was around, except a cat creeping through the hotel gardens near the sidewalk. I pondered the events that had somehow led me to this place and the career I had never expected. Perhaps it was the quiet of the night, or perhaps it was the sounds of the Word of Wisdom being violated in the background, but I was suddenly overcome with a terrible, indescribable emptiness and loneliness—the kind that had gripped me only in the darkest hours of my life. I was in despair. I felt I was the last person on earth who believed in God and had just found out I was the one who was wrong. I asked myself, How did I ever get here?

Others have experienced such feelings as mine that evening. These are the hours in which all of the meaning of our own life presents itself before us and pulls at our very heartstrings. These are the moments when the path of life takes us through our personal Gethsemane, perhaps over and over again.

That evening I realized that the life I was living resembled nothing that I had once planned or even anything that was truly valuable to me. The deepest part of me ached to understand why, despite years of prayers for the greatest desires of my heart, I found myself in this place, alone, with no family of my own, with no one in heaven or on earth knowing or caring where I was at that moment. Even the angels in heaven seemed to withdraw themselves that night, leaving me pondering my isolation.

Yet in that dark night in the Santa Cruz mountains, from deep within me, I sensed a light. It did not shine brightly through me, bringing with it all the answers and illuminating the dark corners of my mind where many questions lurked. The light did not come suddenly, taking away all the questions that require faith and endurance. Rather, it was a still, simple peace—like a seedling finally peeking through the soil, a peace "not as the world giveth" (John 14:27). It was the peace that could come only from hope.

It was a long time coming, that small light of hope. Many painful experiences in my college years had left me extremely downtrodden and disillusioned. I had made it a policy always to give the appearance of being happy with my life. I had tried to achieve success in my education and career. But truthfully, I was a very unhappy woman with very little faith or hope left.

I still wonder how the Spirit of the Lord got through to me

on that night. Thinking back, I see that in the months previous to that moment I had changed little by little in a million different ways, as I opened my heart to my Father in prayer and allowed myself to be taught by the scriptures and words of the living prophets. There is a scripture in the Book of Mormon that came to mean a great deal to me: "Wherefore, whoso believeth in God might with surety hope for a better world, yea, even a place at the right hand of God, which hope cometh of faith, maketh an anchor to the souls of men, which would make them sure and steadfast, always abounding in good works, being led to glorify God" (Ether 12:4).

As I looked toward heaven that evening and only silence returned to me, I felt within my heart the truth of the message of that scripture. I could not see him or hear him or touch him, but I did believe in God with all my heart. I was at a loss to explain how I came to my particular situation in life, which was devoid of many of the opportunities for which I had been beating the bushes for the past several years. But I was completely reassured that because of my belief in my Father in Heaven, I could indeed hope for a better world than the one I knew at that moment!

Despite the emptiness and pain of that hour, I found hope from my faith in the Savior. He was the anchor to my soul. He was the One who made it possible to find that better world. He gave me the strength to endure and remain steadfast even when the meaning of my life escaped my understanding. Elder Bruce R. McConkie stated: "The greatest truth known to man is that there is a God in heaven who is infinite and eternal; that he is the creator, upholder, and preserver of all things; that he created us and the sidereal heavens and ordained and established a plan of salvation whereby we might advance and progress and become like him.

"The second greatest truth in all eternity pertains to the divine sonship of the Lord, Jesus Christ. It includes the eternal verity that he was foreordained in the councils of eternity to come to earth and be the Redeemer of men [and women], to come and ransom [them] from the temporal and spiritual death brought upon them by the fall of Adam" (*Brigham Young University Speeches of the Year, 1980* [Provo, Utah: Brigham Young University, 1981], 79).

Finally, because of my belief in God and my faith in the Savior, I could humbly bow my head and choose to obey and accept their will for me. I could yield everything that was in me, everything I had, and everything I hoped to have to the Father and the Son because I trusted them more than I trusted myself. They knew well the better world that I was seeking; therefore, I trusted that they knew better than I did what I needed to experience in order to get there. After all, my thoughts were not their thoughts; my ways were not their ways (see Isaiah 55:8).

Standing there in the darkness, I learned that no matter how bleak the outlook at the moment, I could still choose to hope for a better world and thereby experience peace. I would never have learned this great truth had I not previously spent hour after hour on my knees, studying the scriptures, and going to church even when I thought I would burst with the pain of the emotions that were stirred there. The fruit of my labors was peace. Slow, still, quiet peace somehow found its way through all the chains around my heart.

Today, the circumstances of my life have not changed. Outwardly, my life looks the same as it ever did. Fortunately, however, the circumstances of my heart are entirely new. As I continue to believe and to keep the Lord's commandments, the little light inside me grows just a bit brighter. The peace that comes from hope is making me ever more sure and steadfast. I pray that I can continue in good works, be led to glorify my God, and praise him with my gratitude.

Heather Hippen is a management development trainer at a financial services company in Salt Lake City. She holds a bachelor's degree in psychology and a master's degree in organizational behavior from Brigham Young University. She has served as a teacher and as homemaking counselor in Relief Society.

Daily Peace

KRISTEN SHUMWAY

It happens occasionally, when he comes home from work, that my husband addresses me as "Grumpy." I acknowledge with relief and chagrin that he notices. On those occasions he will take our two-year-old and our nine-month-old and retreat to the bathroom. On their way up the stairs, I hear him explain, "Mommy feels a little grouchy, but you can still have fun in the bathtub."

I'm not always sure why I become discontented or where the frustration comes from. I feel like an innocent bystander who has been drenched by a gargantuan bucket of water in a slapstick comedy. Once soaked, it takes me a while to regain my usual happy composure. Nevertheless, grumpy or happy, I make an honest effort to fulfill my responsibilities. I feed my children. I try to keep them clean and teach them useful things. I try to be a good wife and a good person. My challenges seem very small and very ordinary. I think it should be easy for me to find peace. After all, things don't change much from day to day.

Unfortunately, it's not that easy. Hormones, spilt milk, and my daughter's developing independence have the uncanny effect of releasing the "mommy-monster." What's worse, sometimes I can't blame my madness or melancholy on circumstances. Things around me are fine, but I find myself in a huff—with no idea how I got there or why. I only know that I have to get help if I want to be happy. (That might seem obvious, but I had to learn that it is not as much fun to stomp around on the self-righteous/self-pity warpath as it is to feel happy.)

19

Yet the bad days have not been all bad. They have taught me (and they remind me) that peace is a daily activity. It's not necessarily a daily struggle, but it has to be a daily priority. That is because peace is a particular blessing and doesn't happen by default. Peace is not merely the absence of noise and turmoil but the presence of the Spirit.

Once I went to Hawaii, leaving Utah's desert snows to bury my car in the long-term parking lot. As soon as I stepped out of the airplane, the weight and moisture of the humidity overwhelmingly proved the change of location long before I saw, heard, or tasted anything. At first I felt almost suffocated, but after an hour or two I began to enjoy the balmy breeze and the sunshine-in-suspension. Having never experienced such a difference before, I didn't know it was so vast.

The peace the Lord blesses me with is at least as tangible as the Hawaiian air. When I first started recognizing it, I was always surprised that I would have such a blessing for an ordinary day. But I've learned that peace is the staple of a successful day, as necessary as air.

Sometimes, though, I still lose that feeling of peace. It usually happens when I become too busy or spiritually complacent. When life is free of major tragedy, too often I assume I have peace. I assume that the steady march of days without trauma indicates my favorable status with the Lord. But it's not long before I have one of those days when I feel grumpy, empty, frustrated, and unhappy. Only then do I realize I've been circulating in an eddy. My peace was only quiet, and I am alone, directionless, and uncomforted.

Thus, even though I lead an ordinary life, I must still earnestly and constantly seek peace. There are many things I can do to show the Lord I want this feeling. I pray daily (in the morning especially). I try valiantly to read scriptures daily. I often write about the things I learn, which fills my mind with extraordinary ideas to ponder through the day. I serve in my callings as well as I can, and I try to be a consistent visiting teacher.

It's not that I do any of these things with a special flair. I do them as well as I can. But I do them because experience has taught me that they help me feel worthy to feel peace. By thinking the thoughts and doing the service required to complete my assignments, I align my desires and actions with the will of the Lord, and suddenly I ask with greater faith for his blessings.

Faith is really the key. I never thought that faith had much to do with peace, but I'm learning that it has everything to do with it. I used to think it was my obedience that brought peace. Peace came when I completed my checklist of righteous things to do as if it were a gumball that dropped out with the payment of the correct change.

But now I think that when I am obedient, I have stronger faith that the Lord wants to bless me with peace. And when I ask for peace with that kind of faith, he can grant it to me.

That kind of faith gives me peace today. It gives me hope for peace in whatever future I encounter. And, miraculously, it enables me to find peace in the past. When painful memories of sins and mistakes jump into my mind, I cling to my faith that I have repented and nothing can overturn the Savior's atonement. Faith allows me to avoid suffering again for repented sins and frees me to move forward, thinking even of the past with peace.

Peace is the promise of the Lord. It is his calling card, his enticement, his confirmation, and his congratulations. It is his gift to those who love him and seek him. And I know, if the Lord is pleased with me, he will always send peace.

Recently a sister I visit teach lost her job. Things are tight, and she and her husband have just had a baby. Although she wants to stay home with her daughter, her income is necessary. When she lost her job, she was optimistic that the Lord was working in her life, making a way for her to stay home. She hoped she would find new employment that would allow her to work from her home. She wrote letters, sent out applications, and ordered job information from mail-order companies. Time passed, and the job she prayed for did not materialize.

When I spoke with her on the phone one evening, she said she was thinking about contacting a company she had worked for previously. She had been quite unhappy there, but she was confident they would hire her again. Then she dismissed her idea, saying, "I can't believe I would even consider such a thing."

As I listened, I remembered the hope and peace she had felt at first, though she had taken her loss of employment very personally. The passing of time was wearing on her faith, and the mounting financial stress was overshadowing the peace the Lord had granted her. We talked for an hour, and by the time we hung up, she was more upbeat. She had fought through the clouding problems, until she could again feel the peace she knew was there.

It was a miracle, in a way, because nothing had changed, at least temporally. All her problems were still leering at her, her efforts were still fruitless, and her hopes of staying home were still dreams. And yet she found again the Lord's gift of peace. Not that it had left her; she had just stacked other things on top of it. Her honest effort to seek it, to remember it, and to reinstate it was her vote of confidence in and acceptance of the will of the Lord. And he was pleased.

When I hung up the phone, I began thinking of people I could call. Who might know of a job? I had already called the Relief Society president—she wasn't home. I went through a mental list of employers in the ward and anyone else who might have contacts. I thought of several, but then one particular brother's name came to my mind. I had to smile. He was a great guy, but he didn't meet any of my criteria. The only reason he seemed to come to mind was that he had lost his job the previous year and found employment through another brother in the ward. He was in sales in an excavating business. How could he help my friend find work in data entry?

It didn't take long before I realized I was being prompted to phone him. His wife answered and told me that he was outside playing in the snow with his children. I didn't really want to interrupt him for such a wild question, so I told his wife the situation and asked if she knew of anything. Of course, she didn't, and I'm sure she, like me, wondered why I would call her husband.

But still, I felt hesitant to hang up. I hadn't really made the call I had felt prompted to make. I was relieved when she said her husband was coming in. When he got to the phone I explained why I was calling, complete with the disclaimer, "I'm not really sure why I'm calling, but your name came to mind."

He didn't even pause. "Yes, actually I do have something she could do. My brother-in-law and I are putting something together. What is her name? I'll call her tomorrow."

To me it was a miracle, sacred and exciting. The Lord knew what this man was planning, even though his wife wasn't aware of the opportunity. Several weeks earlier, the Lord had blessed my friend with peace, and even though challenges had arisen for her in the meantime, the Lord's peace was still there, quietly waiting to be validated. Now her peace is also a testimony.

When I feel an assurance, the quiet and unexplainable knowledge that everything will be well, that I will have strength to endure, it is my responsibility to keep that peace foremost in my mind. I already know I can trust it because the Lord is the source. To keep the feelings of comfort that accompany his assurance, it helps to record the experience or relate it to a friend. That way I am more likely to be reminded that the Lord has spoken to me and that he will come through.

And so I progress through daily life, often feeling the sweet "Hawaiian air" of peace and sometimes losing it, but with renewed determination, rediscovering its richness. And because the Lord truly wants me to be happy, he blesses me again and again with peace.

Kristen Oertle Shumway is a homemaker and the mother of three children under the age of four. She served a mission in South Africa and graduated from Brigham Young University in clothing and textiles. She and her husband, Sheldon, serve together as stake missionaries.

I Am Not Left Alone

CHERIE RASMUSSEN

When my husband, J. R., accepted a job in San Francisco thirty years ago, I thought I had found the perfect life. I would be living near one of the most glamorous cities in the world, enjoying many cultural opportunities, and for the first time in my life I would have enough money to buy almost anything I wanted. I was married to a wonderful man, and we had two beautiful children. After eight years in the workforce, I finally would be able to realize my dream of being a full-time wife and mother. I had everything I had ever wanted, and I thought nothing could spoil my contentment. I was still young enough and naive enough to believe that life was always fair.

We had been in California only about two years when J. R. and I took a group of young people to Huddart Park to camp and play volleyball. During that evening, J. R. began to stumble and lose his coordination. He thought maybe he was coming down with something, but when it happened a second time a few weeks later while he was running, he decided he should see a doctor. After many months of painful tests, his neurologist very bluntly told him he had multiple sclerosis, for which there was no treatment and no cure.

We were both stunned. J. R. was an outstanding athlete in top physical condition. I couldn't accept the diagnosis. We had been married only a few years, and it just wasn't fair. My perfect world was shattered.

Over the next few years, J. R.'s health deteriorated rapidly. He lost the use of one leg and then the other, first using a cane

24

and then crutches and finally a wheelchair. He was hospitalized many times. Yet he continued to work. He would come home from work so exhausted that all he could do was eat and go to bed, and still he insisted on working as long as he was able.

In 1976 he suffered his first major heart attack. He was hospitalized for seven weeks. When he finally came home, he was a quadriplegic and completely dependent on me to take care of all his physical needs.

We were both faced with experiences and circumstances that would test our character. J. R. faced his loss of mobility and his constant pain with quiet dignity and courage. I wasn't quite so noble. I was often impatient, self-pitying, and angry at the unfairness of it all. It took a long time before I realized that if the Lord healed all sickness and prevented every tragedy, we would not have the great miracles that occur when we lose ourselves in the service of others. With acceptance and perspective, we committed ourselves to living as normally and as fully as possible. J. R. was not able to take out the garbage or mow the lawn, but the emotional and spiritual support he constantly gave me more than made up for it. He was my best friend. He listened to me and understood my heart. He believed in me and made me feel I could do anything. To have a husband who loved the Lord, who was forever patient, who loved unconditionally, and who never belittled me was priceless. I quit looking on what I didn't have and focused instead on what I did have.

What a difference that change in attitude made! I felt loved, understood, and at peace. The Lord blessed us both with the determination to live with dignity, and we learned together to put our priorities on our eternal goals instead of on earthly and material wants. We learned to be cheerful during adversity, not just for the sake of others but for ourselves. Bearing our burdens with a light heart brought that perfect brightness of hope. I like to say that I was born and raised in Ogden, Utah, but grew up in Sunnyvale, California.

We learned that life isn't meant to be easy all the time. Everyone faces challenges, temptations, and what sometimes seem to be insurmountable odds. At other times daily demands can so distract us that we lose sight of our eternal goals. A talk by Elder Richard G. Scott reminded me that many of life's disappointments come from looking beyond the mark, from seeking success and happiness where it can't be found.

J. R. passed away in the summer of 1994. A few days after his death I took his patriarchal blessing from the drawer and reread it. I had read it many times before, but this time these words leapt off the page: "Your guardian angel will have charge concerning you and will bear you up in your trials." For the first time I read with real understanding. The Spirit bore witness to me that I had been prepared to be that guardian angel. I am so grateful that the Lord found me equal to the task and used me in this way. In the months since J. R.'s death, I have sensed the loving arms of the Savior around me. He has given me the energy, resources, and strength to do the things I need to do.

Faith and hope are growing things, and in our growing together, J. R. and I focused on the promise made to Joseph Smith: "My son, peace be unto thy soul; thine adversity and thine afflictions shall be but a small moment" (D&C 121:7). I have found this promise to be true. The last thirty years do seem as a small moment. I remember in the quiet moments of life, in the spaces between milestones, only the joy of being together, the happy times that we shared, the moments that made us complete.

I have no idea what the future holds for me, but my faith and hope are sufficient for me to know that I am not left alone. The Savior will give me enough light to take one step at a time. Paul described how "tribulation worketh patience; and patience, experience; and experience, hope" (Romans 5:3–4). Hope helps us to walk by faith, faith that we are his sons and daughters and that we can borrow his perfection until we gain our own. His atonement and resurrection made it all possible.

Cherie Rasmussen serves as Relief Society president in her ward in California. She is the mother of two and grandmother of five.

"Be Still and Know That I Am God"

MERCEDES WIEDERHOLD

I am now forty-two years old and have spent the larger part of the past year in bed. My life has followed a pattern set by Heavenly Father: "To every thing there is a season, and a time to every purpose under the heaven. A time to be born, and a time to die" (Ecclesiastes 3:1–2). This is my season for reflection and study, preparatory to becoming "anxiously engaged in a good cause" in the spirit world (D&C 58:27). I ask myself, Has my time here on earth been well spent? Have I found joy and peace? It is quite easy to have peace and harmony in our lives when beauty and the bounties of life are in abundance. But when trials and hardships arise, it is much harder to find the spiritual salve that will heal the wounds of the soul.

When I was a small child growing up in Mexico, my grandmother owned a pharmacy. Her services as a lay doctor were used by both rich and poor. She used a particular cream that came in a small tin container. It was white and had the consistency of lard. It didn't smell much better. But it was the closest thing to magic. It was prescribed for Mario's diaper rash, for Lalo's injured knee, and even for old Mr. Acosta's rheumatism. It wasn't expensive, and so it was available to all. Our neighborhood had its very own balm of Gilead.

During my childhood, I experienced turmoil and sometimes very difficult circumstances. At the age of fourteen, I was sent to live in a convent to prepare myself to become a Catholic nun. Three years later, I spent a weekend with my family. It was at this time that I attended my first Latter-day Saint church meeting.

Suddenly my life took an unexpected turn. I was introduced to a new religion, one that made much more theological sense to me. I had accumulated doctrinal questions while studying at the convent, and the young missionaries were answering them one by one. There were no mysteries, just learning opportunities. The gospel plan had an order. Everything and everyone was dealt with fairly and, above all, loved.

The most dramatic change came in my understanding of the Godhead and their involvement in my life. I had grown up believing in an all-powerful, mysterious, unreachable God who was to be feared and, above all, to be held in such reverence and awe that one dare not address him personally but must go through a patron saint. The missionaries taught me how to pray. I couldn't believe their temerity: they not only spoke directly to God the Father but expected an answer from him. My first awkward attempts at communicating brought a sure answer to a heartfelt prayer. I became a member of The Church of Jesus Christ of Latter-day Saints in a tiny baptismal font in Guadalajara, Mexico.

I was hungry to learn. I gobbled up such books as *Jesus the Christ*, by James E. Talmage, and *A Marvelous Work and a Wonder*, by LeGrand Richards. I moved to the United States and attended Ricks College. By the time I celebrated my twenty-sixth birthday, I had a husband and six children under the age of ten.

Our family has been abundantly blessed with trials. Both my eldest son and my beloved husband have had an ongoing battle with depression. Our second son, Ben, has been diagnosed with a genetic disease similar to mine. Thirteen years ago, our beautiful two-year-old daughter, Miriam, was found to have a brain tumor, and after eighteen months of struggling, she was called back to live with her Heavenly Father. Shortly after my daughter's death, I began to experience physical problems. Through modern medical technology and through priesthood blessings, we understood that mine was a long-term illness that would shorten my life. After twelve years, I see my body becoming weaker.

I have truly learned line upon line, precept upon precept. I understand that peace and fear cannot abide in the same space.

Anxiety, anger, and the inability to forgive are the antitheses of peace and joy.

I believe that gratitude is the much-needed miracle salve that can heal our spiritual wounds. When I generously apply the balm of gratitude on a painful spiritual sore, not only does the wound heal but instead of unhealthy tissue, I have much stronger, pliable skin that can withstand inclement circumstance.

A grateful heart makes me teachable, and it engenders faith, charity, patience, a willingness to obey, and an atmosphere of hope. I can focus on what is good in my life and see past my sorrow and pain. The balm of gratitude enables me to be strong and healthy spiritually, so that I can experience a mighty change of heart and "sing the song of redeeming love" (Alma 5:26).

I can see clearly God's hand in my life. I am able to trust in his will. In my darkest moments, Heavenly Father answers my tearful prayer: "[My child,] be still and know that I am God" (D&C 101:16). As I see my wounds being healed and my soul becoming stronger, my immediate response is to help those around me who so sorely need nurturing.

I can boldly testify that the effects of the Atonement permeate my life. When in the dead of the night, I am unable to sleep because of physical discomfort, my thoughts turn to the Garden of Gethsemane. I know I am not alone. He is there. He understands better than anyone else any physical, emotional, or spiritual pain that I am asked to bear. We are in partnership on this project called mortality.

Our Savior exhorts me to have patience and bear these afflictions with a firm hope that I shall one day rest from all my burdens. "Come unto me, all ye that labour and are heavy laden, and I will give you rest. Take my yoke upon you, and learn of me; for I am meek and lowly in heart: and ye shall find rest unto your souls. For my yoke is easy, and my burden is light" (Matthew 11:28–30). The weight of my load comes from poor choices and sometimes just plain ordinary disobedience. Sin is usually so easy to commit but so very hard to deal with in its effects. When I use the balm of gratitude to cleanse the wound left by sin, I find our

29

Savior comes to add his strength to complete the task. Gratitude not only creates in me a desire to forgive, but it also helps me to understand that I am forgiven.

I testify that my Redeemer lives. He has paid the price so that justice might be satisfied. A grateful heart is more powerful than any of my grandmother's magic potions. Peace and joy can be experienced in this life.

During my earthly stay, Heavenly Father has blessed me with his richest blessings. For twenty-six years, I have been given the opportunity to be involved actively in his church. Wherever our family has lived, the other Church members have shown us kindness and love. We know members of our ward kneel down and ask Heavenly Father to bless the Wiederhold family. He has heard and answered their prayers. He has inspired Relief Society sisters to bring us home-cooked dinners. They have not only fed our bodies but replenished our souls. This past Christmas, our family had more cookies, candies, and treats than if ten mothers had been baking for us. A group of my husband's priesthood quorum swooped down on our home and within hours had carted off months of windblown leaves and dead branches that had fallen from recent storms. As I lay on my bed, I looked out the window and saw our bishop in the midst of all this activity, raking with all his might. My heart was deeply touched. I am sure his own yard was full of dead leaves as well.

I have been surrounded by many wonderful friends who have lifted my arms when they hung low. For eighteen years my faithful friend Linda has listened to the still small voice. She knows my needs and meets them even before I fully understand them myself. I have as an eternal companion one of Heavenly Father's most courageous and humble servants. He has shared with me his wisdom, priesthood blessings, and love for our Savior. Our children's testimonies are strong and growing. They have already endured more than many do in a lifetime. They have been equal to the task. Our family understands it is during times of great adversity that our hearts are softened and we are brought to our knees in humble prayer. This is when our testimonies grow and we become one with God.

Like the people in my old neighborhood in Mexico, I too have found my own balm of Gilead. When used frequently and generously to heal my soul's wounds, I have been rewarded with joy and peace.

Mercedes Wiederhold and her husband, Robert Wiederhold, are the parents of Michael, Sarah, Ben, Matt, Joe, and Miriam. Mercedes died in January 1997. She spent her life always doing beautiful things, and she is now serving a mission in the spirit world while her son Ben is serving a mission in Washington. That is the way she wanted it, always and forever serving with a heart full of joy, gratitude, and appreciation.

"Sweet Is the Peace the Gospel Brings"

HELEN M. PLUNK

I remember a day in late 1994 when the Spirit kept poking and prodding at me, but I did not want to listen. I believed that, for me, it was too late: I had done too much wrong, and the Lord would never want me back. But the Spirit did not stop prodding. As I reflect on that period of my life, I marvel that I felt the Spirit at all, because I had not lived so that the Spirit would reside with me. A few months later, my bishop stopped me and asked how things were going. "Oh, all right," was my reply. My bishop is a spiritual man who immediately recognized that all was not all right. He invited me into his office, and we spoke for a few minutes. I told him I was feeling alienated from the Church, that if it had not been for my youngest daughter I would not be attending church at all, and that I was thinking of giving up my membership after she was on her own. He was sorry to hear this and asked if we could speak again the next Sunday. I agreed but left his office feeling terrible. Deep in my heart I knew I could not blame my feelings on anyone else, that what I had done with my life's choices was no one's responsibility but my own. Outwardly, however, I was blaming others in the church for my feelings of alienation and separation.

I was reared in a family that did not attend church, and I was not given any religious training as a child. But I have believed in a Heavenly Father and Jesus Christ for as long as I can remember, and I have always thought of them as separate persons with bodies like ours and possessing a great love and intelligence. When I was twenty years old, my husband and I met a couple who

32

belonged to the Mormon church. I wasn't sure just what that was, but they seemed to be a very nice couple. We started talking about religion, and during one of our conversations they asked if the missionaries could come over to talk with us. My husband and I agreed to see them.

After taking the discussions, we were baptized and became very active in the Church. It became the central point of our lives: we went to church twice on Sunday, Relief Society home-making meeting was held on Wednesday afternoon, and Primary was held on Tuesday afternoons. Friday and Saturday evenings almost always had some activity that we attended. Within a year and a half, we received temple recommends and were sealed in the Logan Temple.

What went wrong? I wondered as I left the bishop's office after that first visit. From such a strong beginning, how did I end up at the bottom of a dark pit, a pit darker than I could ever have imagined? Until that time I believed the pain, sorrow, and darkness I had felt at my sister's death six months previous was the greatest I had ever felt, but my own actions would cause pain, sorrow, and darkness beyond anything I had yet experienced.

When I began to talk with the bishop the following Sunday, I did not want to speak of my sin. I felt what I had done was so wrong and so personal that he would never be able to understand and would condemn me on the spot. But again the Spirit spoke, "Tell him the truth, my child. It's the only way." So I did. I told him everything that had happened over the past several years. The words were hard to get out, the pain so intense as I spoke. But once I'd finished, I felt a sense of relief, a sense of peace. He spoke kindly, telling me that what I had just done showed great strength and that I would be blessed. I felt far from being a woman of strength. I felt I was a coward, a liar, someone who had turned her back on Heavenly Father. How, oh, how could he possibly forgive me?

After a time, there does come a peace, a wonderful sense of being forgiven, an all-encompassing love that is ours when we try very hard to take the steps necessary to return to our Father.

Heavenly Father's plan is so precious, so beautiful and so simple, if only we follow as we have been asked to do. He waits patiently for his straying children to return to him.

But the road was not easy. The first thing I was advised to do was to agree to a disciplinary council. I was told what that would be and was given an explanation of the possible results. I wanted to run, to hide—to be anywhere but where I was at that moment. To face the rest of the bishopric and confess my wrongdoings— how could I possibly do that? I cried, and at first I said no, but the Spirit kept working, and at last I did agree. The four days until the council were filled with pain, sorrow, praying, panic, more praying. Alma describes perfectly what I felt as he tells his son Helaman of his own pain and sorrow during his repentance process (see Alma 36).

Thursday morning arrived, even though I had prayed it wouldn't. I prayed that day as I had never prayed before. "Please, Heavenly Father give me strength to do that which I know thou wouldst have me do this day." A feeling of peace arrived almost immediately, with the assurance that all would be well.

That evening I arrived at the bishop's office a few minutes early and again prayed silently while I waited. Soon the process began. It was one of the most difficult things I have ever had to do, but I went forward because I felt the Lord was directing me and the others present that evening.

At the end of the meeting, as I looked around the room, I was surprised by the love and compassion being shown. Yes, this was a very serious matter, but I did not feel condemned, as I thought I would be. The outcome was a period of time on formal probation: monthly meetings with the bishop; no formal callings; praying daily for forgiveness; reading the scriptures daily, beginning with the Book of Mormon; reading my patriarchal blessing weekly; refraining from partaking of the sacrament; paying tithing. All of this I was being asked to do as well as to turn my back on my previous life and not return to it. I agreed to try and went home that evening with a feeling that Heavenly Father was letting me know through the Holy Spirit that he approved my first step back to the path that leads directly home. In Alma 5:33 we are told, "Behold, he sendeth an invitation unto all men, for the arms of mercy are extended towards them, and he saith: Repent, and I will receive you." I believe that Heavenly Father saw something in me that I could not see, that he knew what I could become, and worked through the Spirit to entice me to repent.

The months that followed were spent reading the scriptures and praying fervently for forgiveness and mercy. I cried as I prayed, thinking in the back of my mind that I could never be forgiven. I read the Book of Mormon every chance I got—at work during lunchtime, at home in the evening. Soon I was looking forward to my reading times and gave up television time in order to read. I went on to the Doctrine and Covenants, the Pearl of Great Price, and the New Testament. I bought several audiotapes on perfection, as well as Sister Chieko Okazaki's audiotapes of her book *Lighten Up*. I listened to them in the car. It was certainly better than what was on the radio! I then purchased tapes by the Mormon Tabernacle Choir and the Mormon Youth Symphony and Choir and started listening to the beauty of the hymns. My visiting teachers and my home teachers were supportive and loving. Their example of love and charity and encouragement became important.

Soon I began to have a lighter feeling in my heart. Prayers were becoming essential to me. I began to feel a real connection with my Heavenly Father and with the Savior. Then came the day that I felt a true feeling of forgiveness. I felt I truly was one of Heavenly Father's daughters and that he did indeed want me back! The tears I cried were tears of joy, of supreme happiness. I had never experienced anything like it before. I couldn't wait to tell the bishop that Sunday!

The bishop was pleased with my progress, and shortly afterward he decided to reconvene the disciplinary council to see if everyone agreed that it was time for my probation to end. What a wonderful day that was as each member of the bishopric expressed his feeling that it was now time for me to return to full fellowship and begin to again partake of the sacrament and participate in callings. Shortly thereafter I asked for a temple recommend interview and received my recommend. I appreciate this blessing in my life as I never have before.

From one of the tapes I have been listening to (I still follow the regimen put in place during my probation), I learned that Heavenly Father does not put us here on earth to fail. He wants us to succeed and to return to him. He wants all of his children back home. He gives us the tools and the promises. It is our choice to use them or not to use them. I can testify that I know of a surety that Heavenly Father knows us individually and he loves each one of us. He is saddened when his children make wrong choices, but his love is such that he will forgive if we are willing to take the steps back to him.

In Mosiah 4:11 King Benjamin tells us that "as ye have come to the knowledge of the glory of God, or if ye have known of his goodness and have tasted of his love, and have received a remission of your sins, which causeth such exceedingly great joy in your souls, even so I would that ye should remember, and always retain in remembrance, the greatness of God, and your own nothingness, and his goodness and long-suffering towards you, unworthy creatures, and humble yourselves even in the depths of humility, calling on the name of the Lord daily, and standing steadfastly in the faith of that which is to come, which was spoken by the mouth of the angel."

I have tasted of this glory, goodness, and love, and it is wonderful!

We have beautiful promises from the Lord if we will but do what he asks of us. And though that isn't always easy and we will not always succeed, as long as we keep trying our best, the promises are sure.

I testify that Christ lives and that he restored his church to the earth in these latter days through the Prophet Joseph Smith. I know without a doubt that President Gordon B. Hinckley is the man chosen by God to be our prophet today and that the Lord works with him and through him to give us the continued guidance we need from above during our probationary period here on earth. My prayer is that each of us will be welcomed back, when our turn on earth is finished, with those wonderful words from the Savior, "Well done, thou good and faithful servant" (Matthew 25:21).

Helen M. Plunk is the mother of four and grandmother of nine. She works as an administrative assistant to her company's president. She serves as a ward and stake organist, Relief Society pianist, and homemaking assistant.

FINDING PEACE
THROUGH PRAYING
AND RECEIVING
PRIESTHOOD BLESSINGS

In the Lord's Own Way

KATHY CALDWELL KNUDSEN

The morning was bright and crisp, and I was having a baby. The labor was short, the delivery easy, and my second son was truly beautiful. I was grateful to be part of the birth miracle and thankful that this little boy had arrived safe and sound.

I wasn't prepared for what happened next, however. They handed me a sweet infant, but when I looked into his eyes, I saw that they were those of an ageless spirit, strong and valiant—a sage, if you will, sent to me from a different realm. I was overwhelmed with the power and dimension of his gaze, awed that I was mother to such a spirit. Then the nurse swept him away. When I saw him again, the penetrating gaze was gone. His eyes were those of a tiny baby.

After twenty years, those few minutes are still clear and clean in my memory. I often reflected on the experience but gave up trying to put it into anything close to words. At first I tried to explain it away, but my soul wouldn't let me. Then with time, I came to believe that I had been given a small but significant gift, perhaps a lifeline, to hang on to when the storms of life raged and I felt a deep frustration with this son.

Time passed busily, and my baby became a sweet, delightful child. A shattering divorce brought teenage years that seemed to turn my lighthearted little boy into a sullen and silent youth. He had always planned and spoken of a mission, and I held on to that, knowing that such an experience would help him regain the light that had faded so dramatically. But nineteen turned to twenty, and a mission was not mentioned.

41

I turned to the Lord in a constant appeal. I knew the soul of my son: I had had a witness when he was born. I begged and pleaded on my son's behalf. I fasted and read. I took out a vendetta against the Lord's refusal to listen, and I bombarded him with my will. I stormed with all my might. When that didn't work, I turned humble and said, "Thy will be done," but I didn't really mean it. Time passed, my sorrow and disappointment slowly turned into a resolve, and when I did bother to listen to the Lord, I heard a very quiet yet powerful message: love your son. Nothing more.

With imploring the Lord comes the temptation to bargain. I promised to attend the temple more, to be a more diligent visiting teacher, a more patient mother, a more nurturing friend, a more spiritual daughter. I bargained with the Lord, and to prove the depth of my desire, I followed through on all of those bargains, all the while still begging him on my son's behalf.

Then, in the sweetness of one early morning vigil, I was flooded with a peace I had never known before. I realized that I had really changed. It was now truly acceptable to me if my son chose not to go on a mission, if he chose never to be active in the Church. I was peaceful; I could feel the Lord's love and his acceptance of my petition. Suddenly it became entirely clear: This test was for me, not for my son. The Lord knew what a special and valiant spirit he was. The Lord was looking after him in his own way. It was I who needed to be taught the lessons of spiritual growth, the lessons of acceptance, the lessons of humility and long-suffering. I needed to remember to trust in the eyes of an ageless spirit, strong and powerful, and in the Father of us both.

I learned my lesson. My son has accepted a mission call. We both continue to be taught.

Kathy Caldwell Knudsen is a single mother of four. An educator and school administrator, she loves to travel and read. She serves as a Sunday School teacher in her ward.

The Gift of Peace

CATHERINE CHRISTENSEN

Bang! The echo of the shot lingered in the air. The military color guard stood strictly at attention as the bugler began his farewell song. I had not thought this day would come so soon. My family, standing together, looked down in silence, each restraining tears as the flag of the United States was lifted from the coffin, folded perfectly, and presented to my father. The day was January sixteenth, the day we buried my mother.

I had been born into what I believed was a typical American Latter-day Saint family. My father was a successful mining engineer, and my mother, eight years his junior, was accomplished in her work as a clinical dietitian. I was their second child, my brother Andy being two years older. My parents were independent, strong-willed people who were hard workers. From my earliest memories, I was encouraged to excel. Consequently, from my youth I knew what I wanted to do, I knew that I had the skill and capability to do it, and I knew that I could be successful and happy.

As I grew, my parents' marriage became increasingly strained. From the time I was about seven until I was fourteen, my father was often states and even countries away from home. I understood, the best a child can, that his absence was a necessary one and admired him all the more for his willingness to work so hard for our family. But times were tight, and my mother was compelled to work two jobs to meet the needs of the family, which now included four children. The separation and financial strain resulted in antagonism between my parents. Even so, my siblings and I continued to be happy for the most part and to do well.

One result of my mother's work schedule was a shifting of the household responsibility. When I was about twelve or maybe a bit before, most of the responsibility for the household fell on my shoulders, and I quickly assumed a motherlike role. It wasn't difficult for me to be mature—I had often been told I was mature for my age. I believed that my spirit body was more mature than my physical body, so the compliments seemed appropriate.

About the time the shift in responsibility occurred, I began searching for a testimony. From a young age I had been intrigued with the concept of God and heaven, but I couldn't seem to find enough time to study the gospel. I thought my search was normal for an adolescent, but I now know it was the exception rather than the rule. I felt very close to the Lord and gained a testimony that he cared for me. Although I was in many ways a mature young woman, I was not prepared for what came next. Just as it seemed that my life was going well and easily, my father told us that my mother had cancer.

I was completely devastated by the aggressiveness of her cancer, but I forced myself to participate in the routine of caring for my mother. My father became her full-time nurse. Her illness brought them together, but the reunion never really healed the wounds of the past. Eventually my father became employed, and the responsibility of caring for my mother fell primarily to my younger sister and me.

Our family had never been emotionally expressive. I had seen my dad embrace and kiss my mother only a few times, and it made me feel uncomfortable. Because of this lack of emotional freedom, dealing with my feelings about my mother's illness and the family situation as a whole was difficult. I relied on my testimony to carry me through, although my feelings of loss were steadily intensifying.

As we approached the Christmas of my senior year of high school, my mother looked better than she had in a long time. She even had the strength to shop for Christmas presents and do the

holiday baking by herself. That Christmas was the best I can remember. The day after Christmas, however, my mother's condition declined severely, and every day brought further regression. During this holiday I read Neal A. Maxwell's book *Meek and Lowly*, which offered me hope as I watched my mother rapidly approaching death. He writes, "Righteous sorrow and suffering carve cavities in the soul that will become later reservoirs of joy" (Salt Lake City: Deseret Book, 1987, 11). I didn't know what lay ahead, but I hoped he was correct and that all of the agony we were suffering would serve some good purpose.

On January twelfth I sat by my mother in her hospital room: she in a coma with a body beginning to deteriorate, and I, a seventeen-year-old girl, experiencing a pain more exquisite than any I had ever known. Here lay my mother, the woman who had labored to bring me life and then labored all her life to try to make my life the best possible. My only regret was that I could not bring myself to utter the words "I love you," as it was so uncomfortable for me.

As the days passed, I often found myself rethinking all that had happened in the past three years. My mother's illness had been difficult for each of us. The devastation and aggressiveness of cancer were horrifying, and I had seen it all, from chemo to radiation to surgery. From the beginning I had struggled to understand the lesson in her illness and had tried hard to be good and faithful to make a miracle happen for my mom. The scriptures were replete with stories of the sick being healed and the dead being raised. I agonized over what more I could have done to help heal my mom. I knew that the Lord loved me and my mom and that he was aware of what was happening. At this time, I was given a blessing in which I was told that he would bless me if I would continue to be faithful and would help me to deal with the searing ache I was feeling. I didn't realize at the time, but the Lord was telling me that he would help me understand. He would help heal my aching soul, and he would help me find peace.

About three months after my mom died, I saw her in a

dream. She was dressed in white and had a serenely joyful smile on her face. She told me she was happy and that I had done well. That was all. I awoke feeling incomprehensibly exhausted and yet relieved. I had wondered if I had done the things my mom needed and wanted me to do to help her. Had I helped her feel loved? Had I helped ease her fears of the journey she was about to take? Had I held and comforted her the right way? Did she understand why I didn't tell her I loved her? In that brief dream, I believe I saw my mom, not just in my mind's eye, but actually saw her because I was in her presence. I needed to hear the few words she spoke. Only two people knew the reassurance I sought: I and the Lord. I was assured that what had transpired with my mother was a part of the plan. I began to understand more clearly than I ever had before that if I would trust in the Lord with all of my being and heed his counsels, the healing and the comfort I was searching for would come.

Early that fall I prepared to leave for my first year of college. I was anxious to begin this new epoch in my life. It was a difficult time for me, however, because a few weeks before I was to leave my father announced that he was going to remarry. I was devastated. Not only was he going to replace my mother but he was moving from the only home I had known to a place I didn't know to marry a woman who wasn't even a member of the Church. Didn't he know that this was a mistake? This new situation only deepened my tender wounds. I spent a few days petitioning the Lord to change my father's mind. I talked with my dad and honestly expressed my feelings and emotions. His response only added to my pain, and I felt truly abandoned. I cried, feeling as though my chest were being slowly torn open. I believed that the Lord loved me, but at that moment I felt completely and absolutely alone.

After a few days of what seemed like hopeless petitioning, I was startled as a voice spoke clearly to my mind during a prayer. Softly and clearly it told me to accept my father's decisions. A powerful new feeling of security slowly washed over me. To describe it is impossible, but it was different from the feeling of being held by a parent or of being loved by a companion; it was safer and more sure and somehow more real than any feeling that I had ever felt. At that time and in thinking about it since, I have come to know that what I felt was the pure love of the Lord for me. In the depths of my soul was a little girl who ached for her mother and felt horribly alone and afraid. I knew unmistakably then that the Lord was acutely aware of that little girl and he would take care of her—that he, the God of heaven and earth, was taking care of me. I have known very few things more surely than I knew that.

As it has a tendency to do, life got busy. I enjoyed my college days. My family seemed to be doing well, and I found myself accepting the new arrangement with more and more ease. My life seemed to be going well—in fact, so well that I could hardly believe it was my life. I still missed my mom and longed to be close to her, but the pain was being replaced with a stronger and stronger testimony of the Lord, coupled with a stronger assurance of his love for me. I also felt that in some incredible way I was actually growing in my relationship with my mother. I began to see her life in new ways. I felt sad for the struggles she had had; I met people who had known her who told me about the woman they had known. She and I were separated, and yet our relationship was growing and becoming stronger.

When I was twenty-one I went to the temple to receive my endowment. As I walked through the temple doors, it was as if I had come home. It was to that place that all the anguish and sorrow had brought me. My struggle had strengthened my testimony and helped me turn completely to the Lord. Attending the temple, and experiencing the covenants made therein, is one of the greatest blessings mortals can know.

What is there to glean from my story? As a seventeen-year-old girl I began to search for meaning in my life's painful experiences. I came to understand that true joy can be born of painful experience. The atonement of Jesus Christ makes this joy possible. The Savior suffered for our sins, and he suffered for our lack of understanding, for our loneliness, for our struggle, and for our pain. The healing of our wounds is a gift given to us because of the Atonement, and finding peace is the realization of that gift.

In the years since my mother died, I have still had times when I ache because of the loss I have experienced, but I know now that as long as I allow the Atonement to operate in my life, I will endure my struggles, have my wounds healed, and find peace now and for eternity.

Catherine Grace Clapton Christensen is pursuing a master's degree in counseling with the University of Maryland. She and her husband, Reed Stanton Christensen, reside in Waldmohr, Germany, where they are on military assignment. She serves as ward choir director and as a nursery leader.

The Quiet Balm of Peace

JEANNE KANE PUTNAM

I had been a member of the Church for only two years and was still new to the scriptures when I heard Elder Boyd K. Packer speak in general conference about the balm of Gilead (*Ensign*, Nov. 1977, 59). That was the first I had heard of it. When he talked about this balm that had power to heal, it seemed there was something ancient and mighty about it. I yearned someday to experience this remarkable substance.

The image that came to my mind when Elder Packer spoke some twenty years ago remains the same today. I perceived an oasis in the distance, green amidst dryness, cooled by swaying palms. Although I could not see them, I was aware of people resting in quiet peace beneath the trees. The air that surrounded this place of calm was stirred by a balmy breeze into a delicate, gossamer elixir that cooled the flesh as it lifted the hearts of the people. This was a place of comfort and respite from a difficult journey.

My life had never had much of this balm. My early years were sad and difficult. A childhood disease paralyzed my legs when I was four. I was hospitalized for a year, separated from my family. Using braces and crutches, I negotiated my world and tried to keep up. During my teens my parents' marriage ended in a bitter divorce. An unsuccessful start at a prestigious university left me feeling defeated. When I was twenty-three, my older brother, just twenty-five, was killed. He had been our family social director and source of energy. Any flickering family traditions that we had tried to preserve died with him.

Six months before my brother's death, I had completed my bachelor's degree in psychology at UCLA (University of California–Los Angeles). Changing universities, persevering, and achieving my educational goal were defining events for me. They confirmed that a small light of inner strength and self-worth endured within me. This glimmer of tenacity often dimmed but never died out. It guided me toward the hope I needed to overcome circumstances.

When I investigated The Church of Jesus Christ of Latter-day Saints at age twenty-four, I hoped that the families, marriages, and stellar lives I saw at church would someday become a reality for me, too. I desperately wanted to be part of a functioning family. I married the young man I had been with for several years, whose family was in the Church. We were married in a civil ceremony, hoping to put our lives on track. I was baptized shortly thereafter, and he was rebaptized a few months later (he had fallen away from the Church in his teens).

I married for a sense of belonging to a family, but even as I made the wedding arrangements, my heart told me I was settling for someone who might not be right for me. I wrote off those feelings as prewedding nervousness. I believed that no one else would ask me to marry him; this might be my only chance. A deep-seated, lingering sense that I was less desirable than other women propelled me down the aisle.

At first, we tried hard in the marriage. We were active in our ward, and in two years we had a beautiful baby girl. I resigned from an excellent job to stay home and care for our child. Soon after I gave up my corporate benefits and financial independence, my husband escalated his derision of me. A cycle of threats and other abuse took hold. Incidents of physical violence and unrighteous dominion ensued. He took my name off our checking account and angrily removed the telephone from our house because I did not answer it while I was nursing the baby. Finally, rather than purchase health insurance, he bought expensive sporting equipment.

Bickering, yelling, and contention were daily, toxic reminders of how wrong things had become. When our daughter began to talk, it was clear she understood the ugly mood of our household, and it upset her. Only in the face of her distress could I admit to myself how I had sunk in my expectations of life. Even after unsuccessful marriage counseling, it took realizing that our daughter would be subjected to growing up in such a negative environment for me to decide the marriage had to end.

Finally, the nightmare was over. Or so I thought. The following seven years proved similarly difficult with numerous court hearings, custody issues, legal bills, and the inherent strains of single parenting and working. Nevertheless, the spirit of contention did leave our home. I could kneel peacefully in prayer. And, as it came quietly to heal my wounds, I discovered the balm of Gilead.

I found it while rereading the New Testament cover to cover. I longed for the gift of knowing Christ as promised in Doctrine and Covenants 46. I studied the scriptures verse by verse, made acquaintance with the people in Jesus' life, learned his path, watched his mission unfold, and felt his divine power. Throughout my reading of the scriptures I was often overcome by the Holy Ghost bearing witness of Jesus Christ directly to me. Jesus' love for me was real. I felt it. This intense experience of finding deep meaning in the scriptures remains with me. My longing to know him was fulfilled. Loving him and his apostles, especially John, were golden gifts of balm.

Balm came from callings that allowed me to serve in Primary, Young Women, and Sunday School. Each calling taught me the gospel as if I were a student in those age groups. In each position I grew as a teacher and a leader.

A Relief Society lesson about the blessings of the priesthood taught me that I could seek God's healing blessings for my daughter even when no priesthood bearer was available. This I did on several occasions in the middle of the night. I held her little body and asked Heavenly Father to let her fever drop, or her ears to stop aching, or her vomiting to end—and they did. Peace came to a frightened young mother alone in the darkness.

Gilead's balm blessed my generous, loving baby-sitter, who cared for my daughter while I worked. Each day when I drove to the baby-sitter, I was leaving my daughter in Gilead. How I wanted to be the one to teach and soothe my child; but when I could not, my remarkable sitter did.

The soothing balm was ever-present during court custody proceedings. Court officers were required to gather information from my daughter's schools and teachers, from our neighbors, and from my employers. When the custody evaluation was complete, the court found me to be an exemplary mother rearing a bright, healthy little girl in the face of many challenges. These findings on my behalf were direct consequences of my choices to live according to the gospel and serve Jesus Christ.

After a stake conference at which Elder LeGrand Richards spoke, I shook his hand and introduced my fiance, who was not LDS. Elder Richards took note of the man at my side, leaned over the rail by the pulpit, and said to me, "Remember the temple. Remember the temple!" He said it with such force that I was speechless. I will never forget the penetrating look from his eyes into mine as he repeated again, "Remember the temple." That counsel was from a special witness of Jesus Christ—a fixed gaze from a watchful shepherd. Not long afterward, I ended my engagement. Elder Richards had taught me to expect to marry a worthy man in the temple, to set my sights higher, and I did.

A few years later, I received my own temple endowments after an inspired, caring prophet of God emphasized that worthy women, married or unmarried, could receive the ordinances of the temple and take the temple blessings back into their homes. Placing my life in proper order and entering the temple doors one beautiful September day brought comfort and peace beyond words. The blessings were so extraordinary as to be incomprehensible at first. Sweet unction to my soul.

Later, at a time when things felt very hopeless, while I was kneeling and crying deeply in prayer, the balm of Gilead enveloped me. Alone, again, I was fearful about ever finding a man I could love and who would love me in return. After pleading to my Father, in a quiet moment, I clearly heard, "I am preparing someone for you." That answer restored my wavering faith. I no longer feared the future but knew to live as best I could and trust that all would be well.

Professionally, I did well enough to buy a small, old house in a nearby town. I was in terror during the process of making the purchase. I would drive over to the property and sit in my car, hoping my future neighbors would not see me, and stare at the house and wonder if I was doing the right thing. My fears were quelled during a prayer to my Father (in my car, no less) in which the Spirit said to me, "This is where you should be." After that, I was able to sign the closing papers.

The balm smoothed the transition into my new ward, where I learned that a certain man there, a fairly recent convert, was a wonderful, kind person admired by the ward members for his diligence as the Young Men president. While watching him prepare the sacrament with those boys, I began to understand that he was the man prepared for me and why this was the place where I should be—just as I had been promised. In less than a year our lives were linked together in the house of the Lord, bonded with the sealing balm of the covenant of marriage for time and all eternity. I hope Elder Richards was watching.

Since my marriage in 1987, I have sent my beautiful, now grown-up, daughter off to college, earned my doctorate in clinical psychology, produced an award-winning videotape about what it is like to have a physical disability—and felt secure in the knowledge that I have been guided through all of this.

So where is Gilead? It is east of the River Jordan, southeast of the Sea of Galilee. It is the wooded highlands from whither came Elijah, a land of flocks and spices. And what is the balm? It is ointment from the highland trees, a precious emollient, costly because of its magical soothing of ills.

But for me the balm of Gilead is like the oasis breeze that surrounds and soothes a parched soul. It is the unction of redemption from pain. It anoints with healing, soothes physical aches, and calms worried hearts. It is the ointment of oneness with the healing hand of Jesus Christ, ever-ready to reach out, silence storms, chase demons, and answer midnight calls from young mothers with sick babies. The price of the balm of Gilead is high, they say, but to me it seems abundant and, strangely, free for the asking. The balm of Gilead is peace indeed.

Jeanne Kane Putnam serves as a teacher in Relief Society and teacher development coordinator in her ward. She is a clinical psychologist who enjoys writing, traveling, photography, and studying voice. She is married to Kenneth Richard Putnam; together they share four daughters, two grandchildren, and a good life.

"Encircled About Eternally in the Arms of His Love"

CAROL RICH BROWN

I grew up in the 1950s and 60s in a family that knew much love, poverty, and illness. My mother suffered from health problems that made her days painful and challenging, yet she remained patient and was a source of constant peace in our family. My father, who was devoted to her, was sixty-one when I was born. He had reared ten children, been widowed, and been seriously injured in a truck rollover. He remarried after falling deeply in love with my mother. My childhood was a time of financial uncertainty but spiritual stability, for although my father's earning capacity was diminished as a result of his crippling injuries, he taught me when I was young to love my Savior. I came to know Him as the source of all that is good. In my youth He became a dear friend.

When I was seventeen, my kind and faithful father was diagnosed with leukemia. He died two years later, when I was a junior at Brigham Young University and struggling with classes, boyfriends, finances, and health problems. I needed surgery but had no money to pay for it. A week before my father died, he announced to me that he was "going home." He quickly explained that he would soon be returning to his heavenly home and expressed his great love for me before I left his bedside to return to school. He passed away in his sleep a week later.

Frightened and feeling alone when I returned to school after his funeral, I devoted my half-hour walk to and from campus each day to communing with my Heavenly Father. I told him of my fears, dreams, challenges, and concerns. As the days passed, I

55

came to know what it means to be enfolded in the arms of the Savior's love. I felt him lifting me, comforting me, strengthening me, and guiding me. The Spirit whispered to me that with his help, I would graduate from college, I would be healed, and I would fulfill the mission that had been outlined for me. I rejoiced in the peace and serenity that filled my life. Through the Savior's grace and much hard work on my part, I graduated magna cum laude in three years and began working on a master's degree in education. During those four and one-half years, I came to know in whom I trusted and learned I could rely on him without reservation for guidance, comfort, and strength.

Because I experienced such an outpouring of peace and love from my Savior throughout my college years, I determined at that time to consecrate my life to him. Shortly after I made that commitment, I met the man whom I would marry. As I prayed about the decision to marry Ken, I felt both my Heavenly Father's and my earthly father's approval. I married Ken in the Salt Lake Temple on a beautiful, sunny day in February 1970.

Sixteen months after we were married, the company at which Ken was working declared bankruptcy. I was seven months pregnant. Somehow we managed to survive on the meager income of the minimum-wage job Ken found. Our precious Melanie was born in August 1971, and we were delighted to be parents. Ken secured a better job shortly after our daughter was born, and although we barely had enough to pay for our rent, utilities, and food, we experienced the bounteous blessings of peace and joy that come with paying our tithes and offerings. We later were able to move into a small home. Although tithes and offerings, including temple fund and building fund, consumed more than 25 percent of our meager income, we were content with our simple furniture and second-hand clothing. It was a time of inner growth, a time when we came to know how much we were willing to sacrifice financially for the Lord. We found it easy to return to him some of the bounty he had given us. Although many of our neighbors had higher incomes, we felt happy with the material blessings we enjoyed. We realized we had "enough and to spare" (D&C 104:17). It was a privilege to contribute our Christmas money to build the Jordan River Temple. We also learned we could forego new clothes to contribute to the building fund. In fact, I took our daughter to sacrament meeting in a nightgown because I could not afford fabric to sew her a dress. And yet I was content, knowing I had given all that I could to build up the kingdom.

Ken was soon called to serve in the first of several bishoprics. I discovered that although giving money to the Lord was easy for me, sacrificing my husband was much harder. For the next ten years, Ken served almost continually in a bishopric, either as a counselor or as a bishop. I remember vividly a summer evening when I was entertaining my three young children while Ken was working with the Varsity Scouts on a service project. I watched several fathers on our street playing with their children, and I felt angry and forlorn. Hearing my neighbors' laughter and watching their children's joyful faces heightened my feelings of self-pity and gloom. Finally, in total despair, I knelt in my living room and pleaded with my Father for help. "My children need a father," I cried out. "Why must I rear them alone while my husband devotes so much of his time to serving others? Why do you expect so much of me? Why have you left me alone with such a heavy load?"

Almost immediately, his Spirit spoke to mine. It was the most powerful and clear answer to prayer I have ever received. He said, "I have never left you alone. I am always here to help you rear these precious children. For this season your husband will be serving others who need him. Lean on my arm while he is gone. I am always with you."

When Ken returned home that night, he told the children and me about an aged widow whom the Scouts had served. They had worked in her yard during the evening, and when they left, the sister cried tears of gratitude and hugged each of them. I looked into the eyes of my children as they heard their father's words. I knew they had been better served than if he had been home, for they had learned something of sacrifice and consecration and love. They had seen a tired father leave home that night and an energized father return. We had experienced peace.

After our fourth child was born, the pediatrician told me that our son had severe health problems and would probably be mentally handicapped. David was almost four when he said his first word, and I spent much of his first five years holding him, reading to him, and caring for him as he bravely endured sometimes incapacitating pain, countless doctor visits, and excruciating tests and surgeries. As he grew older, on many days he was too ill to attend school, so I tutored him at home. A cheerful, patient child, David taught me that I could find peace in the midst of uncertainty, and I grew to treasure the time we spent together.

Although my husband promised my son in priesthood blessings that he would be made well and that he would eventually speak clearly and serve a mission, I grew less hopeful with each passing year that these blessings would be realized in this life. Then at David's eighth birthday a remarkable change took place. He began to eat without distress. His gray pallor faded, and a rosy glow appeared. His words became more distinct. Suddenly, he had the energy to play, to attend school regularly, and to enjoy his childhood more fully. I had witnessed another miracle performed according to the Lord's timetable and according to his tender mercies and loving kindness.

Since David's recovery, I have continued to feel my Father's sustaining influence through a series of adversities. I have battled severe health problems in recent years as I served as stake and later ward Relief Society president. I have felt the anguish of caring for my ninety-year-old mother as she has patiently endured the hardships of a stroke. I have known much pain and illness and suffering. But throughout these hard times, I have been encircled in the arms of loving friends and have learned much about compassion, understanding, and mercy. I have poured out my heart to my Father in Heaven in prayer. I have felt his love through the kindness and Christlike service of others. When I have been too weak to walk, he has carried me; when I have been too weary to stand, he has held me in his arms. I know the reality of his pure and perfect love for each of his children. I have discovered that he loves me just as much, if not more, when I am sick as when I am healthy, when I am weak as when I am strong. I have learned that even though no one on earth may perfectly understand my grief or my suffering, my Savior does, for not only does he know what I am experiencing but he has experienced every pain, sorrow, and grief that I have ever felt or will ever know. Because of my adversities, he has become my dearest friend.

Although I would never have chosen any of the problems I have faced, I am grateful for them because through them I have come to know and love my Heavenly Father and his Son. As I have been encircled in the arms of my Savior's love, I have discovered a peace that "passeth all understanding" (Philippians 4:7). I know my Father lives and that my Savior suffered and died for me and for each of us so that we might live again and so that he might "know according to the flesh how to succor his people" (Alma 7:12). I have come to realize that there is no trial, no pain, no heartache, no disappointment that he does not understand and that he has not borne. As I survive and grow from adversity, I am learning better how to serve my brothers and sisters, my neighbors, and my friends. Although I am far from perfect, I continually feel my Father's perfect love for me as I seek to become more like him.

Carol Rich Brown is a homemaker, freelance writer, and tutor. She and her husband, Kenneth S. Brown, are the parents of four children. She has served in Relief Society, Primary, and Young Women ward and stake presidencies and now serves as a Primary teacher.

Only After the Trials

NANCY NANCE

As a teenage convert to The Church of Jesus Christ of Latter-day Saints in 1962, I did not have the grounding in the gospel to realize how vitally important it could be to marry within the Church. So at nineteen I chose to marry my long-time friend, Larry. We were young and starry-eyed until the realities of adult life settled in and we realized we were very different people with very different interests. On Sundays I went to church, and when I returned home, Larry would have gone somewhere to do something "fun." He resented my being committed to anything but him, and I resented his not being committed to what I was committed to. Contention grew between us as we each became more and more miserable. I began to wonder if we had made a disastrous mistake. After some agonizing prayer, I picked up my scriptures, randomly opened them to 1 Corinthians 7:13–16, and read: "And the woman which hath an husband that believeth not, and if he be pleased to dwell with her, let her not leave him. For the unbelieving husband is sanctified by the wife, . . . but if the unbelieving depart, let him depart. A brother or a sister is not under bondage in such cases: but God hath called us to peace. For what knowest thou, O wife, whether thou shalt save thy husband?" I didn't know how long the wait would be, but I knew my prayer had been answered directly.

Three years later, we had our first child, a boy. Three years after that, he was joined by a sister. When she was eleven months old, I had a miscarriage. About three years later I had a second miscarriage. I was getting the message that my body might not be able to carry another baby to full term. We had been married for thirteen years, and our "baby" was almost seven, when I realized that I was expecting again. I decided to call in the heavy artillery early this time, so I asked my wonderful, caring home teacher to give me a blessing. In the blessing he assured me that all would go well. In about a month I began to have the too-familiar problems accompanying a miscarriage. I asked my home teacher for another blessing. This time he administered to me. It was a beautiful blessing, which said in part, "At the end of this pregnancy you will have a normal, healthy baby to hold and to love, and you will forget all the pain you have gone through. You will have a positive attitude about this problem, and this will be instrumental in bringing Larry into the Church." The blessing brought much comfort, but I worried a little about the "bringing Larry into the Church" part.

That same day, early in March, I went into the hospital and lost the baby; however, because of the new ultrasound equipment in the hospital, which no one could read properly yet, I was pronounced still pregnant and sent home to stay in bed. After two months of bed rest, I went in for a check-up with the doctor. He informed me that he was sorry but I definitely was not pregnant. Needless to say, I was shocked. In grief and frustration, I asked him for names of adoption agencies. Relieved that he was now off the hook, he gave me several names of agencies to contact.

Even though I was devastated, I was thrilled to get out of bed and go about the business of taking care of my family. We got busy planting a late garden. The person who was really devastated, however, was my home teacher. He told me he just could not understand. He said, "Nancy, sometimes when my kids are sick and I give them a blessing, I say that everything will be all right because I just want them to get better. But that is not what happened with your blessing. I knew everything was going to be okay." I assured him that everything was all right and that maybe we would have an adoption under way soon. But secretly I was really worried now about the "bringing Larry into the Church" part of the blessing for sure.

One evening during the first week of June, Larry told me he

would like us to sit out on the patio because he had a confession to make. My heart skipped several beats before we were seated on the patio. Larry said he had been taking the missionary lessons on his lunch hour, was about to make a decision, and thought I might be interested. He said that after the latest miscarriage I had maintained such a positive attitude that he felt he needed at least to try to understand the gospel. I was ecstatically happy, yet I felt completely numb. I kept thinking I had heard his phrase "because of your positive attitude, I am going to join the Church" somewhere before. Larry was baptized a member of the Church in July. He has since been a bishop and is serving now as president of our ward's Young Men. Since he became a member of the Church, it has been all I could do to keep up with him.

Within the week after Larry's "confession," the doctor's office called and said that the doctor needed me to come to his office because he had something he needed to talk to me about. I immediately assumed I had some dreadful disease, so I asked the nurse to tell me what it was about. She whispered into the phone that she thought it was about adoption. An unwed, teenaged mother-to-be wanted him to find someone to adopt her baby. Her family supported her decision. The baby was due October 3, and the doctor wanted to know if we would be interested. Interested? This was an answer to prayer! We had questions that needed to be answered, but I assured the doctor that we could muster some interest. We contacted a lawyer, arrangements were made, and the wait began. We didn't mention the matter to anyone else for fear that it might not work out. By October 3, my anxiety level was off the charts. Nothing happened. October 10 came and went, and still nothing. Finally, on October 18, the lawyer called to tell us that a "normal, healthy" nine-pound, thirteen-ounce baby boy had been born that day and he would contact us about when we could pick up the baby from the hospital.

The amazing thing about this was that the due date for the baby I had lost was October 18 or 20. So, "at the end of [my] pregnancy," I had a normal, healthy baby to hold and to love and did indeed forget about all the pain I had been through. We picked up our son from the hospital on October 20 and named him after my husband's missionaries, who had taught him on his lunch hour and kept his secret as long as they dared. Our son is now eighteen and has been a wonderful son to rear. I feel he is truly a spirit special enough that Heavenly Father wanted us to know ahead of time about him and to truly prepare for him.

At the time we got Doug, we learned later, I was one week pregnant. This baby was due on July 5. The pregnancy was almost normal. My two older children, now ten and seven, were excellent help as I geared myself up to caring for two infants. July 5 came and went, but no baby. On July 16 I went into labor. During each contraction, the monitor showed that the baby was in severe stress. I kept thinking, "Yes, there is a problem, but they'll work it out. Women don't lose babies during childbirth anymore." My husband kept saying, "Something is wrong with your machine—you need another machine!" My doctor and his partner were on another floor performing surgery and were not clearly informed of our emergency. Two hours later, the baby's heart stopped, and two hours after that I delivered a stillborn baby. I held him only one time. The death of a child is one of the greatest trials I have ever gone through, but just one month later we had the joyous blessing of being sealed as a family in the Manti Temple after fourteen and a half years of marriage.

During all that time, I came up with the philosophy that has been my balm of Gilead: the Lord won't send me a trial I can't handle. He has told me in the scriptures that he won't. If I have a trial, I can handle it—it's my job to figure out how. God, being who he is, knows not only that I can handle it but how I will handle it. My purpose for being here in this life is not to prove anything to him but to prove to myself who I am, what I'm made of, and that I can overcome trials. With his Spirit to lean on, I am stronger than I ever could have been on my own.

Nancy Nance is a homemaker and mother. She and her husband, Larry E. Nance, are the parents of five children. She serves in her ward as the Relief Society education counselor, a name extractor at the family history center, and a choir member.

The Peace Which Passeth All Understanding

DIXIE DRAWHORN BAKER

Life was wonderful. I had finally finished our daughter Kelly's wedding dress, which had taken me months to make. She had spent the past four months at home after being away at school for three years. That had given us some very special time together as we planned for her wedding.

It was Mother's Day, 12 May 1991. In three days my husband, Lloyd, and I would fly to Hawaii. Our daughter's wedding would be on Saturday, May 18. One week in Hawaii. Wow! We planned to squeeze in a little celebration for our twenty-fourth wedding anniversary while we were there.

Lloyd was still at the church taking care of his bishop's duties when the phone rang. "Mrs. Baker, this is Utah Valley Regional Medical Center in Provo, Utah, requesting permission to treat your daughter Mindy." (Oh goodness, what did this mean? She had only a few days left on crutches after her knee surgery.) "She has fallen and is unconscious, and we need your permission to treat her."

The phone call was a surprise but not a shock. Heavenly Father, in his merciful way, had prepared us for this experience. When Lloyd gave Mindy her name and blessing as an infant, he had tried three different times to bless her with adult blessings, but he was not able to utter the words. We had a great fear that she would not live to adulthood. We kept that heavy burden to ourselves as we watched for hazards in her life.

Mindy regained consciousness about six hours later, after a priesthood blessing. By midnight that night she had had a CT

64

(computerized tomography) scan and an MRI (magnetic resonance imaging). We had spoken with the neurologist and the neurosurgeon. The doctors were 98 percent certain that she had an inoperable, malignant brain tumor with a spiderlike shape. The medical term was *anaplastic astrocytoma*. The biopsy was scheduled for Thursday. I could be in Provo by then. Mindy would remain in the hospital till then, and my sisters would stay with her.

What was left of the night, after that final midnight phone conversation with the doctors, was spent with my mind whirling with questions, plans, and sorting. I had already arranged for our four younger children to stay with friends during our trip to Hawaii. So the hardest part of the planning was done. Lloyd asked, "Dix, what do you want me to do? I'll do whatever you want me to." I answered, "I'll go to Provo for the brain biopsy. You go to Hawaii and be father and mother of the bride."

Until I boarded the plane, I really hadn't had time to ponder all that had happened. I realized from the beginning that this would be a unique experience and tried to embrace it with my senses finely tuned. I felt that there was a definite purpose in my having such an experience. I wanted to be constantly alert so that I would know just what Heavenly Father's purposes were. I felt strongly that I was to learn things that not only would help me grow but that would enable me to help others. How many gospel seeds could be planted with people we would meet who had never heard of the Church? These desires were validated when I was given a blessing in which I was told that people would be watching my example.

During that first week in Provo, I left the hospital after kissing Mindy good night and read my scriptures before retiring myself. I was in great need of the strength and guidance they offer. There were big decisions to be made, and my husband was thousands of miles away. I was traveling in uncharted territory; I didn't know a thing about brain cancer.

One night I discovered a scripture that I could not remember reading before. It was Doctrine and Covenants 88:125: "And above all things, clothe yourselves with the bond of charity, as with a mantle, which is the bond of perfectness and peace." It gave me a clearer understanding of why my blessing had said that I should treat others as though the situation were reversed. I was in the ideal position to exercise charity, and I desperately needed peace. At that moment, I determined that I would conduct myself in a manner worthy to obtain the blessings promised by this scripture.

Despite our earlier premonitions, there was no doubt in my mind that Mindy would live through the cancer. She had received a blessing at age eighteen that promised her that she would live a long life upon the earth, that she would have the faith to be healed by the power of the priesthood, and that her life would be preserved in childbearing. I knew that someone who had celebrated her twentieth birthday two days before the seizure had not yet lived a long life. With total confidence that I knew exactly what those words meant, exercising faith and hope for her recovery was not difficult.

Another factor that gave me comfort and hope was Mindy's attitude. Three days after the biopsy we went back to her apartment for her to recuperate enough to fly back to Houston. As we lay in the dark talking, she said, "Mom, I know there's a mission in all this, and I feel privileged that Heavenly Father has chosen me." She maintained that attitude throughout the chemotherapy and radiation treatments, surgery, loss of her hair, loss of the use of her right side, and loss of speech. She was never bitter or angry. She never asked why. Could I be any less brave with such an example?

Referring often to the notes I had made of the blessing I received that first week brought me the most peace. I was told that my life would change, that this was a temporary situation, and that I should search my heart for Heavenly Father's will. I had been very concerned about how I was going to take care of the rest of my family while being so heavily involved with Mindy. I was promised that I would have the strength to respond to the needs of our other children when they cried, "Mother, where are you?"

Heavenly Father is so kind in the manner in which he gives us the opportunities to grow. The massive task of caring for Mindy, transporting her one hundred miles a day to the cancer center, and caring for our other children came at a convenient time for our family. We had children who were old enough to take care of responsibilities at home. We could afford the gasoline and the six dollars for parking at the hospital each time. The time that Kelly and I had spent in strengthening our relationship before her marriage softened the blow of missing her beautiful Hawaiian wedding. The outpouring of love and help from our ward and community gave us strength.

These things convinced me that Heavenly Father knew exactly what our situation was and how he could ease the pains and apply his balm to our lives. I am grateful for the way in which he gave us this marvelous opportunity to grow and then sustained us through it.

To help us cope with our situation, our oldest daughter, Heidi, gave us the audiotapes of Elder Neal A. Maxwell's book, *All These Things Shall Give Thee Experience.* I learned from him how God's omniscience works in our earthly existence: Heavenly Father knows exactly when and how we can progress and tailors our trials individually. Elder Maxwell explains that if we truly realize that God is omniscient and knows what is best for us, we will someday thank him for the stretching of our souls. Even though I accepted this principle in theory, I still had to learn its practical application.

Mindy died on 12 December 1992, nineteen months to the hour from the time she suffered her first seizure that Mother's Day in her student ward. I had expected that she would be healed until the minute she drew her last breath. How could I now reconcile her death with her blessing that she would live a long life on this earth?

For a time I couldn't. I finally had to accept the truth that there are some things I will not understand in this life. That's just part of Heavenly Father's plan. I discovered that the peace he sends in place of complete understanding makes the trial something you can tolerate. With time the trial becomes a blessing.

Experiences like these give us the opportunity to show ourselves how strong we are, how we can be gracious in suffering, and how we can glorify our Heavenly Father, even when we don't understand his purposes. We reach into our hearts and yearn to understand the part of the Savior's atonement that concerns his suffering for our sorrows, not just for our sins.

Peace came for me when I received specific guidance and strength through a priesthood blessing. It came when I truly realized that our separation at death is a very temporary thing. And it engulfed me when I realized that Heavenly Father not only tailored this trial for my growth but walked with me through it.

Dixie Drawhorn Baker and her husband, Lloyd, are the parents of seven children. A full-time homemaker, she has volunteered on the public library board, in parent-teacher organizations, and in foster care. She serves as stake Primary president.

FINDING PEACE
THROUGH SERVING

Choosing to Enrich the Lives of Others

CAROL K. ANDERSON

The day had been long—not unusual for a Sunday—and I was not happy when the doorbell rang. I ignored it but waited to hear the barrage of rings demanding answer. When that didn't happen, my attention increased. I wondered if the caller was still there. I was one of those tired Latter-day Saints who wishes for a "do not disturb" sign, but whoever was on the other side of the door didn't know that. At first I heard the chatter of children and a woman's voice hushing them. Then I heard the shuffle of small feet dancing against the cold. I went to answer the door.

The sun was sinking, and the cold startled me. I looked out the door. Four small, emotionless eyes looked back. Children shouldn't be out when the wind is miserable and snow creeps into everything. The youngest of the two girls didn't appear to be more than three. She held up in one scruffy hand a plastic bag, the kind you put sandwiches in. Her other hand was holding a gold-colored necklace toward me. My glance at the bag full of necklaces and the one being shoved in my direction for a closer look was interrupted by the woman's voice: "Five dollars each." She prompted the girls to say more. I could have said I don't buy things on Sunday, but even if it had been Thursday, it wouldn't have mattered. Instead I explained it had been a busy week with children selling candy for school projects and the Scouts collecting canned goods for the Drive against Hunger. The woman quickly apologized for intruding and motioned for the children to leave while she thanked me for helping the food bank.

Were they hungry, or was someone sending them out for

71

money for the next can of beer? From their appearance I guessed no one really loved any of them very much. "May the girls have a treat?" I asked. The woman hesitated and then said yes. Selling necklaces door to door in a plastic bag couldn't be lucrative.

I went to the kitchen looking for snacks: peanut butter crackers and cheese crackers, lemon cookies and chocolate cookies. I made a point of giving them plenty each, hoping the feeling of desperation inside me would stop. The girls were eager to discover the different kinds each package held and managed crackers, cookies, and steps down from the porch. I closed the door, still wondering. Were these children homeless? Was Mom trying to earn rent money?

When parents have to struggle to provide, it hurts; and the hurt spreads from them to the children. Did food banks help this family? I didn't know. My mind reverted to two Sundays before when the request came from Welfare Square for volunteers to can salmon for the food bank. I was one of the few volunteers. Fish oils, I discovered, never completely wash out of your clothing and shoes.

The balm of Gilead is an ancient physician's formula for healing. It is like the hands of good people everywhere trying to make a difference through service. No one person can prevent or solve all the problems of life. Just the same, one person can choose not to underestimate the ability of an individual to enrich the lives of others. Every time a Scout picks up newspapers for recycling and the proceeds advance charity projects, a Young Woman adopts a single mother to help with child-care, the elderly are included in activities, or a Primary teacher calls on a child who is ill or needs encouragement, good happens and beauty is born again and again.

I find peace when I avoid a laissez-faire attitude. Deliberately abstaining from involvement with those in need is like quicksand. What hurts one person eventually hurts you. It would be great if problems were self-contained, but like secondhand smoke, the effects are unavoidable. What isn't good today gets worse tomorrow.

Moral people know that we are our brother's keeper. Many people are lost in a barren desert, incapable of self-renewal, the water of life never found. Christ walked a land of dry sand, did not halt his steps at the Garden of Gethsemane, withstood the agony of the crown of thorns, and wavered not at his crucifixion.

When people stop respecting themselves and others, confidence and hope die. We all stand near an avalanche; life is unpredictable, and terrible things happen, taking everything with them. But we can stand firm in doing right. Christ, our Savior, asked forgiveness for those "who know not what they do" (Luke 23:34). How many times have we been forgiven? Being perfect, Christ atoned for all mankind. Can we not do something for each other, especially when we don't want to or feel it isn't fair?

Let us all respond to the capacity of the soul to reach spiritual maturity. Do we need tangible rewards, a cheering crowd, or a writeup in the news or the book of the rich and famous? Peace comes from unobtrusive acts of decency and consideration for those in need, who can take courage because of some small act of caring.

Giving to grubby little girls is a small act. Canning salmon isn't glamorous, and the fish oils smell. But the inconvenience is minor. The result of the day's work is the feast at the Lord's banquet. We choose. What a grand opportunity we all have to be in the service of our Lord, the greatest being to be born on this earth, who has invited us to return and be with him forever and forever.

Carol K. Anderson is a volunteer advocate for children and works as a play therapist in community service. She and her husband, Ronald, are the parents of two children and the grandparents of two granddaughters. She and her husband serve together as visiting teachers at local nursing homes and as the historians in their Salt Lake City ward.

His Hands in My Life

KRISTINE ASHTON

One of my earliest memories as a young girl is of waking in the morning to music. My mother is a wonderful musician and would practice very early in the mornings. Often I sat next to her on the piano bench, where I could watch her hands on the keyboard. Occasionally, to my great delight, she would invite me to place my hands on top of hers. This was always a magical moment for me. Instantly, I became a wonderful pianist!

My fascination with people's hands has continued. I notice hands. I am in awe of the many things that our hands do—create, touch, lift, soothe. I have often wished I could place my hands on those of a wonderful artist, chef, or carpenter, so I could magically, instantly, experience those talents.

My husband, Mark, and I were married several years ago in the Oakland Temple. Before the wedding ceremony we sat together in the celestial room. We held hands and talked of the romantic life we envisioned together. We were the only ones in that exquisite room for several minutes. It was a perfect moment. A few years later, as we awaited the birth of our first child, I imagined other perfect moments for my life. I envisioned myself as a new mother, holding a beautiful baby in my arms. I envisioned my husband blessing the baby and then holding him up for everyone to see.

And so I was stunned to learn two days before our first child was born that the baby would require immediate medical attention. When our son, Michael, was born, I heard one little cry and briefly saw his face before he was rushed off to Primary Children's

Medical Center in Salt Lake City, an hour from our home at the time. Two days later I was able to see him up close for the first time. I wanted to hold him, but medical equipment and monitors around him prevented that. I did the only thing I could do—I placed my finger in the palm of his little hand. He held on!

I was encouraged by his strong grasp every time I touched his hand. We are born with this grasp reflex—the ability to hold onto things. It changes over time as we learn not only to hold on to things but to let go of things or to hold things in a different way. I believe that a grasp reflex remains within us—sometimes all we can do is reach out and hold on.

Through my gentle son's hands I learned of the healing power of prayer and that we must pray for one another by name. It seemed as if I prayed constantly for Michael's life, and I did find peace.

The hours, days, and weeks following Michael's birth were truly the roller-coaster ride that family and friends of the critically ill understand so well. The fatigue, the raw emotions, and the uncertainty of Michael's health were heavy burdens. I knew I had to be steady and controlled. I had to watch out for the best interests of my son. But my reserves were quickly depleted—burned up in a flash fire with any negative news about Michael's condition.

During this time—the only time in my life I have honestly done this with daily consistency—I did three things every single day Michael was in the hospital: I prayed morning and night, read from the scriptures, and wrote in my journal. It was such an intense personal effort to do this that I am still puzzled. Why did I focus on those activities? I remember needing the full gospel of Jesus Christ. I remember the plan of salvation and my Savior being tangible. Every other aspect of my life was surreal. Praying, reading scriptures, and writing brought a peace of mind I have yet to replicate in my life.

When I reread my journal of that time, I see with crystal clarity the complete situation we faced. I see through my words how physically tired I was. I see that so many people were concerned for us. My dear father and mother telephoned daily and traveled to be with us. My sister, brother, friends, and relatives visited. My husband's entire family was supportive. But I could not appreciate or process these things in the midst of the hospital roller coaster. I was too distracted by our moment-to-moment highs and lows. My journal became an important source of comfort and perspective.

Michael was the first grandchild on my side of the family. My mother, the wonderful musician, came to visit and care for our new family. Once again I put my hands on hers, hoping for a magical transformation. At her urging, we attended a session together at the Salt Lake Temple. For a few hours I was calm. Later that day the turmoil welled up again. The tide was in, with huge waves of despair crashing over me. The restorative powers of the temple had been unusually brief. Yet, my mother's hands still guided me.

She knew a shortcut from Primary Children's Medical Center to the freeway. As we left the hospital that night and headed for home, she directed me to turn down a steep, hilly street. From the top of the hill, and all the way down, all I could see in front of me was the magnificent Salt Lake Temple, gloriously illuminated. I took that route every night. As I began my long drive home it was with the panoramic view of a lighted Salt Lake Temple vivid in my mind. This spectacular scene gave me the courage to drive away from my tiny son, night after night.

Michael survived a five-month roller-coaster ride. He survived many surgeries. He did come home. He was given a name and a blessing in church. My husband did hold him up for everyone to see. Six weeks later, in a hospital room, Michael passed away as I held him in my arms. My son was beautiful, brave, and strong.

Six years later, I am able to say that I have been given a marvelous spiritual gift. I could not hold Michael as a brand-new baby, but what an incredible experience it was to be with him at his passing. At the most difficult, devastating moment I have ever faced, there was golden brilliance and light. Now I am at peace with that chapter of my life.

My peace was not easily obtained. It came after many tears,

questions, much confusion, and a darkness that threatened to engulf my very being. During this struggle my outward behavior was stable. Inwardly, privately, I was crushed.

I thought I should get over my grief quickly. I thought I should carry steadily on—chin up, pioneer heritage, and all. I wasn't prepared for the length of time required to heal such a wound. Time is the great healer. That was limited solace, as was the saying I grew to deplore: "That which does not kill us makes us stronger." It hurt to be so strong. It hurt a lot. It hurt too much. I was not prepared for the turmoil or for my feelings of emptiness. I didn't want to pray, but I prayed anyway.

When I prayed, I discovered that God seemed to have changed. Where once there had been such comfort in personal prayer, there now was nothing. Silence. Did God still hear me? It was as if he had hidden himself from me. Perhaps we had all retreated to our own corners for a time.

I held on to anything that would fuel my deep hurt. At Michael's funeral a friend announced her pregnancy. That hurt. Then, everyone around me seemed to be producing babies. More wreckage to which I could cling. The question, How many children do you have? was the recurring sore bruise. I grasped at those injuries. I clutched them tightly. They fed and enlarged my pain.

How would I ever heal? Would I ever feel happy again? I had to let go of my hurts. As I began to let go of innocently inflicted pain, I felt the warmth of acceptance beginning to wash over me. I remembered the love of those closest to me. I began to heal. The balm of love is powerful. It soothed, refreshed, and made me whole.

I remembered music. I now play the piano without my mother's hands. A pattern of coincidences led me to my current work, providing music for young school children. The final stitches repairing my shattered heart were sewn by the voices of three hundred singing children. I am "Miss Kristine" to them. Daily they greet and thank me. They are without guile and undue sentiment. Their pure goodness restored me.

Finally, I remembered the art of being good to myself. It is a fine art that improves with practice. A power, refreshing and restorative, does emerge when I create time for myself.

That art of caring for myself is varied. It is a daily walk outside. It is stopping to listen with 100 percent of my attention when a child, any child, speaks to me. It is loving the two young children we have in our home now. It is a ladies' night out for dinner, movies and, best of all, talking. It is a good laugh! It is getting a good night's sleep—meaning that I go to bed at a reasonable hour, knowing the beckoning call of household tasks is better answered the next morning.

It is a trip to the temple, that same Oakland Temple of my wedding. Our hand-holding moments in the celestial room are no longer the soaring, ecstatic dreams of young love. I am firmly grounded by reality. I am firmly grounded by the knowledge that I am a survivor on more than one level. I am firmly grounded by a calm, gentle peace of heart and mind.

It is a tender moment of prayer, the soothing balm of Gilead from a Heavenly Father who is no longer hidden from my view. It is willingly placing my hands in my Savior's to be accepted, loved, and guided forward.

Kristine Ashton is a musician specializing in childhood development through music. She and her husband, Mark, are the parents of three children. She has served in ward Relief Society presidencies and as a teacher; she serves now as a counselor in the Primary presidency in her ward.

"I Will Not Fail Thee, Nor Forsake Thee"

CAROL KENDALL

On Friday, 22 July 1994, a knock at our door changed our lives forever. Two policemen informed us that our seventeen-year-old son, Marchus Christiansen Kendall, had been killed in an automobile accident. He had been miniature golfing with friends, and they were on the way home when the accident occurred. Numbness crept over my body as my husband and I were driven to the hospital to identify Marchus. We were escorted to a back room and left alone with our son. He looked as if he were just sleeping peacefully. They handed me his wallet. It was all he had with him, and I couldn't let go of it. Earlier that day, while helping me pack for girls' camp, he asked me why girls had to take so much junk. I assured him everything was a necessity and if I could take more, I would. We laughed and joked and danced in the kitchen. He even washed the dishes and vacuumed without being asked. My last words to him were, "Be good, and remember who you are."

This was not our first experience with sudden tragedy. In 1987, our daughter Kelli had been injured in an automobile accident. She was in intensive care for two months, and we were told she would not make it. I prayed and prayed that she would be all right, but she kept getting worse. I grew angry because my prayers were not being answered the way I wanted them to be. One night the thought came to me that Kelli was not just my daughter; she was a daughter of her Heavenly Father. He loved her just as much as I loved her, and he would do only what was best for Kelli. It was very painful, but I knew I needed to utter the words "Thy will be done" and truly mean them, placing my full trust in the Lord. From that point on, Kelli slowly improved.

When I had to utter those words again that Friday night in July, it was easier because my faith had earlier been tested and I had learned to be stronger, my faith and love for my Heavenly Father had increased, and I had gained a deeper desire to do his will. Each trial we endure makes us stronger and gives us a greater ability to endure the next one. I learned to "trust in the Lord with all [my] heart; and lean not unto [my] own understanding" (Proverbs 3:5).

Then we had to inform our other children about Marchus. It seemed they picked this night to be at the four corners of the world. Our son Steve and his wife were in Kaysville babysitting for her family. Our daughter Kelli and her husband were camping at Payson Lakes. Our daughter Miquelle was out on a date, and I had to leave a message with her roommate. She didn't know which brother had been killed until she walked into our house. Our son Jon was at a sleep-over. We called in the middle of the night to say we had to pick him up immediately.

As our children arrived home there was an outpouring of love and tributes to Marchus: what a great brother he was, what a great example he was, how he had helped all of us. It was a very private, sacred, and precious time for us. We felt the peace the Holy Ghost brought into our home and into our hearts that night. The Holy Ghost gave us the strength to endure those first days and continues to comfort and strengthen us. I am so very grateful for that blessing because I don't have the strength to go through this alone. Through our trials the influence of the Holy Ghost becomes a reality.

I opened Marchus's wallet when sleep refused to come. I found a well-used *For the Strength of Youth* pamphlet and a seminary card with a picture of the Savior on it and a line from Joshua 1:5: "I will not fail thee, nor forsake thee." On the other side was a sticker that said, "I hope they call me on a mission." Marchus did receive his mission call. It just came a little earlier than we had planned, and it's a little farther away and for a little longer time than we had planned. Like all parents of missionaries, we have read about his mission field. From the scriptures I have learned many things about the place where Marchus is serving.

The next day people arrived nonstop. I had always felt in the past that I might be intruding when I called on someone newly bereaved, but now, receiving such visits myself, I realized that I needed the love and strength that was transferred to me through their hugs and expressions of love and sorrow. The prayers and simple acts of kindness for our family will never be forgotten and can only be repaid in service to others. When I'm having a hard day, I try to find someone or some way to serve. I have learned to pray for those who have to face the same trials as I did without the knowledge of the gospel of Jesus Christ. Each day I have more gratitude and love for my Savior and more love for his perfect plan of salvation and exaltation.

Songs, sounds, and memories sometimes bring tears. People may assume they are painful tears, but in reality they are poignant tears of sweet memories of a loving son. They are also tears of gratitude to a loving Elder Brother, Jesus Christ, who continues to give us strength, comfort, and peace each day.

On 10 January 1996 we took our daughter Miquelle to the Missionary Training Center. I was sure I did not have enough strength to say good-bye to another child. I avoided her all morning because I knew I would break down. But when I walked into the living room and saw her luggage, a wonderful feeling filled my entire soul: luggage meant she would be coming home!

Peace comes through loving the Lord, having faith and trust in his plan, serving others and in knowing that we can and will be together again. Trials and tribulations are never easy, and we don't seek them, but I can testify that our trials have drawn us closer as a family, have strengthened us, and have increased my love and gratitude to the Lord for being at my side and holding me up. The only way to find true and lasting peace is to love and trust the Lord unconditionally. He will "not fail thee, nor forsake thee" (Joshua 1:5). I keep Marchus's seminary card in my wallet to remind me that the Lord has not failed me nor forsaken me, and he continues to fill my soul with peace.

Carol Kendall is a homemaker from Orem, Utah. She and her husband, James D. Kendall, are the parents of five children. She served in Young Women for twenty-four years on both ward and stake levels; she is now a member of her ward activities committee.

Through the Love of Others

JULIE MONSON

In ancient days in Israel many believed that disease was caused by a "dis-ease" with God, that the sick person had been caught by the evil eye. One treatment for certain ailments was a balm used in treating wounds and abrasions. Its unction would heal the skin, and the rich potency of the odor would tell the recipient that the healing process was beginning. The balm of Gilead came from the balsam trees that grew in great abundance in the steep ravines and hills of Gilead in Israel. The sap of the tree was mixed into a salve that was sold as far away as Egypt for use in healing wounds and in warming the skin in sprains and breaks.

The true balm of Gilead came with the Savior and the healing that he brings to our soul with his words and deeds. Those words when listened to and adhered to could wipe away the "dis-ease" with God and open the doors of true healing to the spirit of love and light. The Savior's atonement could enable mankind to heal spiritually, much as the salve from Gilead could heal bodily woes.

Throughout the early years of my life I had unshakable faith in the goodness of the Savior, but events of my life have wrenched me from the course of belief and caused me great "dis-ease" with God. Each child born into our home came under a cloud of travail and threat of death. Each child suffered from unusual and life-threatening maladies. Finally I was told by doctors that I should have no more children and that the child I was carrying had only a 10 percent chance of entering life with normal physical and mental faculties. Those around me rallied to help, and I prayed constantly for the apparently impossible—a healthy baby. I had to stay in bed. The Relief Society provided meals, prayers were offered, blessings given, and soon the wonderful balm of warmth descended from heaven to bless and comfort our household.

There was such joy at the birth of our son when all involved realized that he was normal. One of the most moving moments of my life came when my obstetrician unwrapped this tiny baby at his first postpartum check-up. This fine and caring man began to undress the baby's tiny frame, and as he did so the baby grabbed his finger while the doctor held his tiny foot. I watched as tears coursed down the doctor's cheeks as he whispered, "This is a miracle. There were days when you left that I prayed because I didn't know what to tell you. This baby is a miracle." The balm of love, blessing, and charity had combined to bless my son's life and continues to do so today as he grows into a handsome, intelligent, and complete son of our Father in Heaven.

I believed that these events were my life's big trial. I felt that I had passed the test and now just had to return the blessing by serving others. But what was ahead would be harder, more painful, and more disconcerting than anything else I had ever experienced.

For the first fifteen years of our marriage my husband was deeply involved in state politics. In 1984 he ran for Congress. He won the race, but we lost the battle. In politics the rule is to get elected, build an image, raise money to get reelected, and then be reelected. There is no room for mistakes or regrouping. If you do, you are only walking the race, not running it. So, after an acrimonious and bruising Congressional race, my husband worked hard to keep what he had achieved. We all worked hard. Our family moved to Washington, D.C., with the attendant woes of displacing junior-high and elementary-school-age children. We prayed to find the right way for us. But as time went on there seemed to be no answers or right way. Our eldest son was unhappy and found older friends who led unsupervised lives. One daughter was so miserable that even her teacher suggested that we send her back to Utah for school. Another daughter was having difficulty learning, and testing revealed a serious learning disability. We had to alter the way we were helping her in significant ways. My husband was never home, and Church and home responsibilities were mine alone. On the phone list of a Congressman, the spouse is last. I was overwhelmed, angry, and rebellious. I did not like this test. I slogged through my life, becoming more and more unhappy.

Then the party leaders, senators, and governor decided that in the best interest of the party my husband should not run for re-election. The media grabbed the story, and life became public misery and humiliation. We had no privacy, and only a few friends stepped forward to support my husband.

The disillusionment became overwhelming, and the personal devastation was total. No one was willing to talk openly to us. Innuendo and insinuations were the rule. We prayed and fasted but found no answers. We felt adrift in a sea of politics. Finally my husband announced he would not run again. When he did that, we stood alone in the world. Suddenly, political friends became invisible, and "here today, gone tomorrow" took on a real meaning.

Our future was moving back to Utah and starting over with a family of teenagers and growing children needing larger and larger shoes and more food.

This time there was no balm; depression became my daily companion. Pain and anger became the bywords of home life. I counted my problems instead of my blessings. I could find no good in my life at all. I tried to find the Lord, but the feelings I had about our circumstances got in the way. I hated the politicians I had thought were friends, and I said so. My husband found a job, and we limped along, patching our lives back together. The week before Christmas 1991 his employer told him his job would end in two weeks. This time I landed at the bottom of the pit.

For eighteen months my husband was home sending out resumes while I taught school. He sought some help from political and community leaders, to no avail. The sting intensified one day when we walked down the street and observed some of our old political friends ducking across the street to avoid us. It was as if we were forgotten and unloved, and I felt we must deserve it. Then the anger set in, anger at a world I couldn't understand, anger at unanswered prayers, anger at those with perfect lives, and, most destructive of all, anger at the Lord for leaving me alone.

But the Lord in his infinite wisdom provides strict tutorials, and slowly I realized there was balm for my soul. A bishop was loving and kind, a friend called to say that his family was fasting and praying for us, and small jobs were offered by not-so-famous friends. Those quiet souls, who were also treading with difficulty through life, began to answer our prayers. How? I asked. Then I realized they were in tune with the Spirit. Inspiration was guiding them to find, lift, and help me. The balm had been applied to the wound.

Starting to be able at last to look at things from a perspective of gratitude, I began to realize I had been blessed to receive a teaching job in an elementary school near downtown Salt Lake City. The school had many challenges in touching children's lives. Eighty-five percent of the children lived below the poverty level. There were Tongan, Hispanic, African, Vietnamese, and Caucasian children in the classroom. Many were abused or neglected. Some were heavily involved in gang activities that disrupted learning. In teaching there I had to work hard. My graduate degree was in secondary education, but the principal told me that if I could get into a graduate program for a year, I could be certified to teach elementary school. In other words, I had to go to school to teach. I would teach until three in the afternoon and go to the university from four to ten four nights a week.

Hearing of this, my visiting teachers said, "Hey, we can help." All of spring quarter, dinner was brought every Tuesday and Thursday so I didn't have to worry about my family. I was stunned at their generosity and caring. I was ashamed, too, that I needed help. Help continued to pour in. Checks for large amounts of money appeared to help with our children's school and personal needs. Many times donations were anonymous with a note saying, "We love you." At Christmas our front porch seemed to have been mistaken for the Sam's Club loading bay. Workers appeared one day to clean and aerate our yard. I began to realize that the Lord was asking me to let go of my pride, to accept pain, to forgive, and to realize that love through others' actions is also his gift and balm to the world. Slowly I started to change. I looked at my school class and realized that I could reach out in love to some of God's children in a unique way. For the time they were in my classroom, they could be valued, safe, and loved. I could learn from them the meaning of youthful exuberance and the vitality of the human spirit.

I began to think that maybe the Lord did love me. I looked at my neighbors and friends differently. I had been unable to soothe and fix my family, but they through their righteousness had seen our needs, and those who loved us had quietly stepped in to serve. My anger began to be replaced with awe and a sense of gratitude for unconditional acts of charity. In my daily life I began to see the web of quiet kindness that had been woven to keep me from being lost to my despair and pain. Gradually anger was replaced with gratitude, loneliness with companionship, fear with confidence, pride with humility, and unbelief with the knowledge that God does love me. He was forcing me to give up pride and despair to find my own strength. I began to repeat Moroni 10:20–22 as my daily litany:

"Wherefore, there must be faith; and if there must be faith there must also be hope; and if there must be hope there must also be charity. And except ye have charity ye can in nowise be saved in the kingdom of God; neither can ye be saved in the kingdom of God if he have not faith; neither can ye if ye have no hope. And if ye have no hope ye must needs be in despair; and despair cometh because of iniquity."

I had felt bound by my own failings, which held me tight to despair. I learned to let go, to forgive. I learned to forgive others, to forgive unfairness, to realize that the struggles of life are real and will not leave us. But the Lord will not leave us either. He applies his balm in many ways.

In revealing my great inability to handle the darkness in my life, I find that I cannot despair. There is light, and hope, and faith. That is the balm of Gilead. The Savior is there in so many ways, leading and guiding me without my knowledge. I need to have patience, to be more willing to accept, and to work hard. He suffered far more than I, and yet his pure love directs the charity that must wrap my heart. I realize that peace takes patience, hope, and faith. I am learning.

There is a balm as sweet as Gilead's. It is the sweetness of Christ and the gospel of service that has come into my life. It has helped to heal my heart and will continue to do so as long as I turn my eyes to him. If I clothe myself in the robes of charity, returning to others the gift that has been bestowed on me, then I will have the faith and hope I need to give back to the world the gift of life that our Savior intended for me to share with those around me.

I believe in Christ. He is the Redeemer, the giver of peace.

Julie J. Monson teaches in an inner-city school in Salt Lake City and has served on the boards of several community service organizations. She has been an advisor to Lambda Delta Sigma and president of her ward's Young Women; currently she teaches Primary. She and her husband, David S. Monson, are the parents of five children.

Receiving Peace

N. ANN SNIDER

The balm of Gilead. What an appropriate topic for me at this time in my life! I have finally graduated from college and now face the demands of being a mother to two young sons and of helping to support my husband as he works to meet the grueling demands of a doctoral program. My time and energy are often spent trying just to get through the day. I have struggled to find places in my life where I might turn for peace. As President Elaine Jack has said, "Spiritual peace is in short supply these days" ("Relief Society: A Balm in Gilead," *Ensign*, Nov. 1995, 91).

I have wondered how I might be able to use the healing powers of the balm of Gilead to find that peace. As I have sought my Heavenly Father's help to have more peace in my life, I have been amazed at the ideas that have come through my study of the scriptures and other uplifting materials and through talking with and listening to others.

One such experience came recently when I attended stake conference in the Assembly Hall on Temple Square. President John D. Liddle, president of the Liberty Stake in Salt Lake City, was speaking. During the Sunday morning session thus far, my nine-month-old was convinced that he should be crawling up and down the stairs in the Assembly Hall and trying out every vowel in his already extensive vocabulary (and I had thought that he would sleep). My four-year-old had just tried to go find his friends up in the balcony, taken a tour of the Assembly Hall via the stage where all of the stake presidency and other dignitaries were sitting, and then escaped into the choir seats only to find himself lost. Despite these minor incidents, I did hear President Liddle give a challenge to us in the congregation. He challenged us each day to think of one person we love, pray for that person, keep him or her in our thoughts the whole day, and then, at the end of the day, write down the experiences we had in praying for that person. He said that as we turned our thoughts to others and their needs, we would begin to forget ourselves. He suggested that perhaps as we prayed for people whom we loved and who needed our love, names of people whom we didn't necessarily love would eventually come up on our list, and through our prayers hearts might be softened and feelings of hurt and anger might be healed.

As President Liddle spoke, I felt the Spirit whisper that this would be a great way to add peace to my life and give me someone each day to think about other than myself. Determined, I went home from stake conference and found an old, half-used journal. I told my husband he could start at the back with his names and I would start at the front with mine, and when we had finished that volume, we would continue with a new one.

I thought about all the people I love and concluded that I would start with my husband and sons and move on to other people each day as I felt directed. With all the people I know, I figured this project would keep me busy for years. Surprising things started to happen as I prayerfully added a name to my list each day. I did start with my husband and children, but the names that followed have appeared on my list in no apparent order. For example, one day a friend called having roommate problems. I put her name on my list for the next day. Another day, the mother of one of my son's friends called for advice about her Church calling. She was struggling to maintain good thoughts about some people in her ward, and I wrote her name on the list for the next day. It still amazes me that when I add a person's name to the list, peace washes over me and thoughts come into my mind of things I might do or say to give comfort as my friends and family struggle to live more peaceful lives and find answers to their problems. I believe, as President Elaine Jack has said, "We can soothe a suffering heart when we can't eliminate the trouble. We can bring reassurance and support, kindness, and calm" ("Relief Society," 91).

When I start my day with someone else in mind, my day is filled with the Spirit bearing witness to me of how wonderful that person is and of all the good qualities that person has. By concentrating on the positive, I feel a greater love for that person by the end of the day. My memories throughout the day focus on the happy events I have shared with that loved one.

I have also realized something even more wonderful from this exercise. I have found that peace comes through the mere fact that I am trying to obey my leaders. Elder Boyd K. Packer has said, "Obedience is a powerful spiritual medicine. It comes close to being a cure-all" ("The Balm of Gilead," *Ensign*, Nov. 1997, 60). So, to feel the healing balm of Gilead work in my life, I need to obey my spiritual leader. I also feel that my spirituality has increased because I am now praying regularly and writing in my journal, two tasks that have not always come easily. Elder Packer has also stated: "Prayer is a powerful, spiritual medicine" ("Balm of Gilead," 60). I am beginning to see this as I pray daily for those I love.

On the days when I truly put these principles into practice, I move through my day with a deep calm, in contrast to the chaos that usually is all around me. I also find that I live the gospel more fully and try to obey the commandments of God on a deeper level. Sister Jack has said: "In our families we learn to appreciate the spiritual peace that comes from applying the principles of charity, of patience, sharing, integrity, kindness, generosity, self-control, and service. These are more than family values, sisters; these are the Lord's way of life" ("Relief Society," 92). Thus, living the gospel can bring us the peace we all are seeking.

I have once again discovered the scriptures and begun to apply them as I have been counseled by my priesthood leaders and by my loving Heavenly Father. Through serving in the Church, mainly in Relief Society, I have also uncovered hidden talents and abilities, expanded my knowledge, and become better and stronger than I ever imagined I could be. I live a much more peaceful and happy life as a wife and mother.

John 14:27 often goes through my mind. Jesus says, "Peace I leave with you, my peace I give unto you: not as the world giveth, give I unto you. Let not your heart be troubled, neither let it be afraid." What a wonderful promise.

Yes, there are many ways to find peace. I believe that if we truly seek to do the will of our Father in Heaven, to obey, to serve, and to think about the many people we love, peace will come into our lives.

N. Ann Snider is a homemaker and graduate of the University of Utah in environmental psychology. She and her husband, Daren P. Snider, are the parents of two sons. She served a mission in Germany and is a member of the Relief Society presidency of her Salt Lake stake.

FINDING PEACE THROUGH CHANGING PERSPECTIVES AND PRIORITIES

Look for a Silver Lining

LYNN F. PRICE

The tranquillity of one's life can be shattered by a mere telephone call. Christmas was just five days away when my son called to tell us that his two-month-old son was comatose in the hospital, a victim of SIDS (Sudden Infant Death Syndrome). They were able to sustain him only to the extent that organ donations could be made.

For the next thirty-six hours I cried and prayed and wondered why this precious little infant had to leave mortality so soon. So suddenly! So unexpectedly! So right before Christmas! As I wrestled with my emotions, the Lord caused a sweet, peaceful feeling to come over me, and I knew it was all right. This precious spirit was promised a place in the celestial kingdom and would be denied none of the blessings of mortality. He was a gift, so to speak.

No sooner had this feeling of peace come to me than the phone rang. The baby was being flown to Salt Lake for burial, and my daughter-in-law was calling from Boston to see if someone from our side of the family could speak at the funeral. Her father was willing to represent her side of the family. Because of the spirit of peace I had been given, I could say I would be honored to speak.

Barely five months later, we received another devastating phone call from our son. Our oldest grandchild, a beautiful six-year-old girl with long brown hair and large blue eyes, had been rushed to the hospital and was then comatose. This time the peace I needed did not come so readily. Her life was spared, but

95

she was in a coma for an extended period and in the hospital for three weeks. When she awoke, she had suffered brain damage. She had to learn everything over again: how to walk, how to talk. Adverse reactions to multiple medicines caused her to be critically ill, and she spent another three weeks in the hospital. The brain damage caused her to have numerous seizures, and because she failed to respond favorably to the usual seizure medicines, her family and doctor had to resort to experimental ones. One caused her to lose weight. Another caused her to lose all her hair. Another allowed her hair to grow back. Another caused her to feel hungry all the time.

Today, at age twelve, this dear girl has numerous problems. Part of her brain is that of a normal twelve-year-old. The other part is stuck at age five or six. She cannot read or do arithmetic. She has no friends. Life for her is pretty miserable.

My soul found peace after my grandson's death, but my granddaughter's situation has caused me much sorrow. Tears flowed freely for days and weeks and months. During that time, as I worked around the house, I listened to a recording by the Mormon Tabernacle Choir entitled *The Twenties*. Most of the songs just passed by without my hearing them particularly, but every time "Look for a Silver Lining" was sung, it caught my attention. I finally recognized that Heavenly Father was answering my prayers and trying to assuage my grief. He impressed upon my soul that I needed to look for silver linings.

What silver linings could there possibly be? I considered my grandson's death. First, there was the knowledge that he was saved in the celestial kingdom. Then there were all the kindnesses and prayers offered by friends, family, and associates. My son was a surgical resident, and those over his program were most gracious in allowing him time away during this difficult period. We also developed a great sensitivity for others who have lost a young baby.

My granddaughter's problems present some of the same silver linings. She, too, is promised a place in the celestial kingdom, because the gospel teaches that children who are impaired will inherit the celestial kingdom the same as will children who die before the age of accountability. Her family has moved to Salt Lake City, and numerous kindnesses and prayers have been offered by friends, family, and associates both here and in Boston. In addition, other members of her family have grown in different ways. Her father has gotten involved in school board activities for the disabled. I taught music to her class in her school. I have developed a great love for sweet neighbors who have gone to the school with me to play the piano for this singing time. These sweet sisters have given of their time to help children with whom they have no special ties. They serve simply because I have asked them to do so. People in her ward have also helped. One sister volunteered to be my granddaughter's Primary teacher because this precious child was having such a difficult time in her class.

Through these trials particularly I have come to appreciate the role of adversity in our lives. I used to think that if we tried hard enough, we could avoid having major problems in life. I have learned that that is not the purpose of life. We are here to be tried. We all have, have had, or will have problems that will try our faith. If we do not know sorrow, we will never really know joy. If we stripped everything from our character and personality that we have gained through trials, we would end up with a bare shell of what we are. I have also learned that we will not be judged on what problems we have but on how we handle them. And I've learned that every problem, if we look hard enough, has a silver lining.

I still wish my granddaughter didn't have her problems. But I can't think of any I'd want her to trade for.

The scriptures don't tell us just to hang on by our fingertips. They tell us to be grateful for all things. I believe that also means we should be grateful for the trials that can prove us worthy to return to live with our Father some day. The scriptures tell us to endure to the end, but they also tell us that "men are, that they might have joy" (2 Nephi 2:25). We are told that the

Savior will give us peace, if we trust in him. By finding silver linings to our problems, we can find that peace and joy in this life. I have.

Lynn F. Price is a homemaker, published author, and community volunteer. She and her husband, Richard R. Price, are the parents of five sons. She has written and directed ward musical programs and served in leadership positions in the auxiliaries; she and her husband are the music co-chairs and co-directors in their ward.

The Caterpillar

JUDITH T. URRY

I saw something tumble from the limb of a tree that branched over the stream. It was a fuzzy, lemon-colored caterpillar about two-and-a-half inches long, with huge black eyes. It landed in a heap on the steep, bare incline between the tree trunk and the water. Dark mountain soil made up the bank, together with a few loose pebbles, some early fall leaves, and a gnarled root or two knobbing up out of the earth.

The caterpillar lay for a moment as if stunned. Then it rolled over and resolutely rippled straight up the bank.

I considered its dilemma, decided things looked grim, and told it so. "Little caterpillar, you have almost no chance." Of course it paid no mind but crawled and slipped, crept forward, and then rolled back down the bank. With no pause, it rolled over and began again. It climbed to the top of one of the roots and then fell to the base again. It rolled back over and humped along, sliding on the pebbles but not stopping. It made slow, grubby, tiresome progress to return to the place from which it had fallen.

I asked, "Why don't you retreat to the lower ground and spin your cocoon among the tangle of vines and sticks next to the stream?" But visions of deep snow and rushing spring runoff answered my question.

"What's wrong with attaching yourself to the nearby root? Spin there. It is much less trouble." The answer came just as if the struggling insect were conversing with me. "My cocoon would be easily tampered with so near the path. Safety is possible in the high places only, where my tired, creeping self can rest a while, awaiting the change that winter and spring will bring. Then I will emerge a beautiful butterfly, able to rise above this dirty and painful struggle."

I settled back against the rock by the water, where I had been watching and listening before I saw the caterpillar. Still doubting that it would succeed, I first felt sorry for it and then admired the steadfastness and determination that were carrying it closer and closer to the tree trunk and perhaps success.

"Ah ha," I speculated, "that completely straight tree with smooth bark. What then, Little Fuzzy?"

No answer. The caterpillar just held tight and wiggled its way around and upward. I'd catch a glimpse of yellow as it wound to my side of the tree. The last time I saw it, still moving up, the caterpillar was twenty or more feet up the tree trunk, past three limbs.

I had come to the cool seclusion of the canyon alone and troubled, hoping for healing and peace. On this morning, I felt particularly disappointed and frustrated. I could see that many of my lifelong dreams were not going to be realized. Living had become difficult. I was in midlife, at the point where the fun and excitement of acquiring had changed into the long, lonely grind of dedicated, stick-to-it responsibility. I walked (stomped would be more accurate) up the canyon near my home, angry and close to tears. After a few miles of uphill walking, I found my anger mellowing into a dull, listless ache.

I prayed silently as I hiked along, scarcely hoping for help. Presently, as if in answer to my request, came a whispered direction: "Here. Turn here." Without questioning, I veered off the edge of the canyon road through the trees and brush, making my own path.

A shady glen opened before me, offering a pleasant refuge. I was astonished by the beauty of the spot—the lacy greens of the ferns and other foliage; the wide, shallow stream with its soft murmur; the occasional chirp and call of birds as they fluttered around the tree branches. The sun dappled the stream and the grass. A feeling of safety poured over me, as if a set of protecting arms had wrapped about me, cocooning me from the harshness of the outer world.

I hardly realized I had left my emotional baggage on the rocky canyon road, and for the first time in weeks I felt free of anger and resentments. I settled back on a patch of grass and leaned against an outcrop of granite near the stream. Sitting as still as the rock behind me, for uncounted moments I let this beauty wash over and around me, not trying to think or work anything out. A black oval bug with striking red zig-zags on its back adorned a nearby leaf. Sheer enjoyment dressed my soul.

How long I remained there, I'm not sure, but gradually thoughts came to me. I seemed to hear questions, and I answered them out loud:

"Of course I believe in what I'm doing."

"No. Oh, no. I'm not willing to quit. I want so much to finish. Too much is left undone."

"I know I sound ungrateful. I feel ungrateful when I act like this."

"It's just too hard. Can't I have it easier? Why do I have to struggle so?"

It was then I saw the caterpillar fall, and I watched it for more than an hour as it fought to climb out of harm's way. Thoughts of deception and disappointment in my own life made the caterpillar's struggle my own. My former inability to meet those challenges began to be replaced with resolve to do my own climbing and to do so with the dignity and patience I had observed in the caterpillar.

I had needed to be reminded of my vital commitments, that others depended on me for that which I had to give. And no promises have been made about how easy it would be. A forgotten bit of scripture came to my mind and splashed through my being, just as the sun dappled the grass and stream: "Wherefore, be not weary in well-doing, for ye are laying the foundation of a great work. And out of small things proceedeth that which is great" (D&C 64:33).

This experience was a turning point for me. During the months that ensued, I was able to restore order and a measure of satisfaction to my life.

The following summer, well and coping, I made a pilgrimage to this place so vividly alive in my mind. I searched for the exact spot, walking the stream edge the best I could to locate what I thought had been my refuge. The raging spring runoff of melted snows had caused the stream to cut a new path. Gone were the grass and the underbrush, leaving only the giant cottonwoods that lined the stream—bulwarks of safety for tiny, yellow caterpillars. Completely changed now, the area was exposed to view from the road. The rock I thought I had leaned against the year before was now in the middle of the streambed. I closed my eyes and easily recalled what had been there for me. I knew that what I had found at that place and at that time would remain with me for as long as I needed to remember.

I still meet with disappointment and setbacks on occasion. We all do. Those negative elements of life must be confronted as they happen. The Chinese recognize that in their word for *crisis*. Their meaning is twofold—danger and opportunity. Though there is danger in any situation, there is also opportunity. Sometimes it is not easy to see, but in the long haul it is not what happens to us but how we meet it that counts. I am still learning, and there may come a time again when I'll need an extra nudge to start moving up my own rocky stretch of bare bank.

Meanwhile, that fiercely determined caterpillar is a powerful reminder of how to meet life's challenges. I pray for strength to keep trying, to be thankful for what is mine to experience, and to keep going, no matter how difficult the climb.

Judith Evelyn Tilton Urry was born and reared near Palatka, Florida. A fifth-generation Latter-day Saint, she has served in Primary and Young Women and is now Relief Society president in her ward. She and her husband, Francis M. Urry, are the parents of six children and the grandparents of ten.

Turn to the Light

DIANE L. MANGUM

Sunlight through chapel windows—it was a simple symbol of peace and comfort for me on busy Sundays in a hectic season of my life.

Not very long ago, my six children were small, and my husband was elders quorum president with meetings before church each week. At home, Sunday mornings were a whirlwind of getting children washed and dressed and combed and out the door. No matter how much I prepared on Saturday, come Sunday morning, socks and shoes and hair bows and scripture bags and the one last picture I needed for Primary could all somehow disappear.

When we finally straggled our way into sacrament meeting, hopefully still early in the opening song, I would plop down on the bench next to my husband, breathe a deep sigh, and look to the east towards the windows. Our chapel faces south and the sun peeks over the mountains and through the windows just about the time morning sacrament meeting begins. The amber windows are of textured glass that makes the sunshine sparkle and dance, so even a little light seems bright.

As I turned to those windows after a harried Sunday morning, I saw the light and felt at peace. Worship could begin now for me. God was still in his heaven. The flurry and frustrations of the last hour could be put aside, for the sun would dance across combed and uncombed hair alike. I had gathered my flock and we had made it to a safe haven for at least a few hours.

But then January came, and we had afternoon meetings

instead. It was easier to get to church on time, but when I walked into the chapel I was disappointed. The morning sun had already shone through those east windows and moved on.

I'm a little slow, and so it took me a while to adjust. Nothing stays the same. Change is an inherent part of life. But then I discovered there are west windows in our chapel, too. All I had to do was look the other way to see the same sun dancing and feel the same reassurance. God was still in his heaven. All was still right with the world. I just needed to adapt to new circumstances.

Light through meetinghouse windows is perhaps a trivial concern, but the principle I learned from it has become valuable. I am the agent responsible for finding my own peace. The Lord is constant, even though life is not.

Mine are mortal and frequently lazy perceptions of life. I usually think that what is comfortable is good. I want peace to mean the absence of conflict and frustration. I want the good days—when my children are laughing and smiling and we are all together—to last forever. I don't want heartache or worries. I'm afraid of trials. And when I think of peace, in my mind I see calm water, stillness. I want peace to mean finding a good place in life and then holding on tight to it. But I'm learning that stillness is an impossible illusion. It doesn't work anymore than holding on tight to just one secure place on the iron rod will get you to the tree of life. There is no escalator under our feet that will transport us to peace. We have to do the moving ourselves.

Life is not about stillness. To grow is to change. Righteousness cannot even exist in a vacuum. To be righteous is to face choices and conflict. To have joy is to know sorrow. Peace is not about the storm that is absent. Peace is about the storm that is weathered.

A couple of years ago, some very quiet and personal events swirled through my life to rob me of peace. The daily events of home and children marched on. I still did the laundry and cooked dinner and went to meetings. But in the quiet, dark moments of the night, or when the house was still and I sat alone on my bed sorting socks, my heart was filled with more anger and frustration and distress than I had ever known. How could God let these things happen? I wondered.

Some people face a serious event that robs them of peace. For me, it wasn't just one thing. It was the layering of several things. Any one of the several things that troubled me would have been enough to rob me of peace, but why had all of them come at once?

It began to be important to me to keep a mental list of my trials. In fact, part of my daily routine was to review the things that troubled and tormented me. Faster than my phone number I could recite the list to myself. Not only that but I hung onto that list and wore it as if it were a merit badge I had earned. Grief such as mine, I assured myself, was not easy to come by. I needed to keep track of every point so the gravity of the situation could be properly assessed. Others might not be able to see the trouble in my soul, but I knew that the Lord knew. And I went to him with my list of complaints, like a schoolchild tattling to the teacher and waiting for instant restitution. I prayed for peace, but I didn't want to turn my head and look for the light. Stubbornly I held my ground and asked that peace come to me—after all the trouble I had had, surely I shouldn't have to go searching for it!

As I mentioned, I'm a little slow to realize some things, but finally I do learn. I learned that it doesn't matter if all the angels in heaven are bending down to give you a hand if you won't reach up to take hold. I learned that there is nothing in the world heavier to carry than a list of troubles. I learned that storing up your grief brings no awards, only weariness. I learned that I don't need to carry anguish. I can set the whole list down. I can reach my hand up. I can turn my face to the light.

Conflict, disappointment, trouble, and change all come to each of us because we came here to grow. Peace is not about stillness. It is about the constancy of the love and comfort of the Lord. God is still in his heaven, and whether we choose to share in it is up to us.

Interestingly, I found that finding peace is not like receiving a vaccination. We can't get a single shot of it and then assume all will go well. I have found that peace in one's heart is more like manna in the wilderness. It needs to be gathered every day. But it will always be there as abundantly as we need it.

Many sisters among us bear great burdens and have endured the sorest trials—the loss of a spouse, the loss of a child, the inhumanity of war, the indignity of terrible crimes. I know that the Lord weeps with them and offers great comfort.

Life is sometimes hard for many others of us as well. Sometimes it is not a single event that makes our hearts heavy. Sometimes it is the accumulation of small things. I know there is an inclination to suppose that God has more important concerns than our small worries and fears. We may even get so carried away that we believe part of our trial is not to ask for help because that would be akin to complaining. I have sometimes felt that way, but I don't think that supposition is true. What is true is that sometimes we need simply to relinquish the stubbornness that keeps us from turning for help.

We don't have to wait for the wounds of the soul to be deep or serious before we seek comfort. The soothing balm of Gilead is sufficiently plentiful and the possibility of distress is sufficiently available to warrant looking for peace every day.

We can find peace when Sunday mornings are frantic.

We can find peace when we don't want to face uncomfortable change.

We can find peace when we are worried about our children, when we aren't sure how we'll find the money to repair the car, when our temper is short and our list of demands is long.

We can find peace when there is conflict around us.

We can find peace even when the grief sits in our chest as if the weight of the mountains were upon us.

The Lord can help us move mountains.

The only secret to finding peace is remembering that we need to turn to the Source of it. When circumstances change, we need to be willing to turn our faces again to the light. And when we are in the wilderness of life, we must gather the manna of comfort every day. It won't keep for us on the shelf. But I know that if we go to the Lord to ask for peace, the angels of heaven will stoop down for as long as it takes to give us a hand if we will reach up to take it. And the soothing, quiet comfort that we seek will be ours.

Diane L. Mangum is a homemaker, freelance writer, and Gospel Doctrine teacher in her ward Sunday School. She has written two books and published articles in the Church magazines. She and her husband, John K. Mangum, are the parents of six children.

Obligation or Opportunity?

TRISA MARTIN

Discouraged, I juggled my squirming baby, his diaper bag, and five Singing Time posters in my arms and hurried toward the door. "Wasn't that lesson marvelous?" women's voices murmured as they left Relief Society. Smiling weakly I tried to echo agreement, but my mind whirled in turmoil. Why don't I feel marvelous? I wondered. All I feel is overwhelmed with obligations.

Each Sunday my burden grew as I added to a growing list of requirements for a faithful Latter-day Saint woman. Over and over I heard, "Read the scriptures, go to the temple, pay your tithing, fast every month, magnify your Church calling, write in your journal, research your genealogy, hold family home evening, teach your children, serve your neighbor, be a missionary, grow a garden, build your food storage, live the Word of Wisdom, cook nutritious meals, keep up your job skills, do your visiting teaching, etc., etc." Exaltation, I believed, was reserved for those valiant ones who managed to do everything on this list.

I worked hard at perfection but always fell short. Six young children demanded most of my time, and my weaknesses got in the way. Instead of being wise, however, and not running faster than I had strength, I kept adding to my list. By trying harder and being better organized, I should be able to do it all.

To improve my skills I attended a workshop on time management. The teacher showed us how to set realistic goals and plan our time. He also cautioned us that everyone has limits. When we choose to add another activity to our busy lives, we should eliminate something. His advice made sense, but which worthy obligation could I eliminate?

Attending church became a struggle because I didn't want to hear any more things I should do. No one guessed the internal battle between my idealized vision of a Latter-day Saint woman and my less-than-perfect life. Then I mentioned my concerns to a friend. "I understand how you feel," she said. "Sometimes my non-LDS friends seem happier and more at peace. They're not burdened by a big list of obligations."

Living the gospel was supposed to bring me peace. So why did I feel so anxious? Peace is freedom from internal conflict or anxiety, a state of tranquillity. How could I find that tranquillity? After sincere pondering and prayer, I received my answer: gospel obligations are opportunities to find peace.

In 1994 the Primary theme was "The gospel of Jesus Christ can bring me peace." For the children *peace* was defined as a feeling of love and safety and quiet that comes from the Lord. I asked myself, When do I feel love and safety and quiet? The answer came: When I am living the gospel.

Reflecting on my life, I can see how the gospel has always brought me peace. As a teenager who didn't date often, I struggled with self-esteem. My belief that I was a daughter of God built self-confidence. The promises in my patriarchal blessing gave my life direction and sustained me when I felt discouraged.

Two years after my marriage, my father was diagnosed with stomach cancer. Throughout the long year of his illness, I prayed often that he would get well. His death shattered my faith for a while until I received a spiritual assurance that everything would be all right. This witness and a belief in life after death brought peace after a devastating loss.

As a mother, I experienced priesthood blessings that comforted me when my children were ill or injured. I felt peace during stressful times: when my newborn struggled for life in the intensive care nursery, when an eleven-year-old son smashed his bicycle into a car, and when two teenage sons rolled the car to the bottom of Big Cottonwood Canyon.

The gospel has brought peace to the lives of my family and others. It has been an anchor for my teenagers, missionaries, and college students. It sustained my widowed mother as she served as a temple worker and gives hope to my aging mother-in-law. To a young neighbor fighting leukemia, the gospel brought courage and united our ward in service and prayer.

Years ago as a college student, I spoke with a young man who was investigating the Church. "What will you do if you get to heaven and find out it's all wrong?" he asked. After thinking for a moment I replied, "I believe the gospel is true. Everything the Church teaches will help me become a better person if I live it."

I still believe what I told him. Everything on my list of obligations will improve my life and help me find peace; yet in my quest for perfection, I misunderstood the gospel. I saw it as an overwhelming list of requirements beyond my abilities. Living the gospel in its simplicity, however, means loving God and loving my neighbor. Every obligation and opportunity rests on these two principles. Every day I can love God by praying, studying the scriptures, and loving others. All other obligations are worthy opportunities to implement after prayerfully analyzing my circumstances and defining my limits. I cannot do everything all the time, but if I keep trying, over a lifetime I can accomplish many things. Doing my best is all that matters, and only I and the Lord can determine what my best is.

With a young family, perhaps I can only read scripture stories with my children and do genealogy by visiting my grandparents. Compassionate service might mean caring for my own children. Raising a garden might be growing tomatoes in a planter box. Buying a few extra cans of food each week could build my food storage. A Primary calling might be a chance to learn the gospel by teaching children. Missionary work may be accomplished by being a good example to my neighbors or writing to missionaries. Visiting teaching might be a time to build friendships. Going to the temple could be a peaceful opportunity after a hectic day.

What about my life today? How do I find peace? I live the gospel in simplicity, accept my weaknesses, work bit by bit at overcoming them, and congratulate myself for all the good things I do. Then I pray for help and keep trying to find opportunities.

Last Sunday when I left Relief Society, I carried no squirming baby and no guilt, only my scriptures. My children had matured, and so had I.

"Wasn't that a marvelous lesson?" a friend commented. "It made me want to work harder on my genealogy."

"Yes, it was," I agreed. I didn't feel anxious because my genealogy isn't finished; rather, I praised myself for starting my mother's life story and writing in my journal. And I felt peace.

Trisa Martin is a freelance writer, published author, and state treasurer of the League of Utah Writers. The mother of six children, she has taught elementary school and worked as a PTA president. She serves as organist in her ward and as a stake missionary.

Father, I Am Yours

DIANA J. KENNARD

*This is my glory, that perhaps I may be an
instrument in the hands of God.*—Alma 29:9

I am not an essayist. I'm not even very clear on what an essay
is. It sounds terribly structured and academic, but when I read the
theme, "Balm of Gilead: Women's Stories of Finding Peace," I
thought, Stories I can do.

Peace. What a great word. What a great feeling. I remember
what great peace I felt when I gave away all the size eight and
smaller clothes I would never wear again. Great peace came in
knowing I had finally conquered the eating disorders that put
them in my closet in the first place. Peace came in knowing I was
loved because I am me—and that was enough.

I'm finding this whole peace issue is greatly related to giving.
Whenever I give things away to Deseret Industries, I feel great
peace that I don't have to store it anymore. I felt great peace
when I gave up my job to become a full-time wife and mother.
But the greatest peace I have ever felt was when I gave away my
talents, my hopes and dreams, my fears and frustrations, my home
and family, my life, my love, my heart, my soul, every fiber of my
being to my Lord and Savior Jesus Christ.

So, how do you do that? Do you simply walk out the door and
never look back? Draped in a saffron colored sheet, do you sit by
the road in the classic lotus position chanting *om?* I don't think
there are any formulas. All I can do is tell what happened to me.

Paul and I were married and had four beautiful children. Life was going along wonderfully. Then one day the most unthinkable thing happened. Paul came home from work and brought everything from his office with him. This was something I never thought would happen to us. We were out of a job. Now it was crunch time. We needed money. There must be a way for me to make some money to help out. Should I go back to work?

Years before, after six years of trying to have children, we had made a covenant with the Lord that if he would send them, I would stay home and take care of them. Now we had four of his elite, and I was starting to panic. Paul was in shock. He quickly found work but at one-third his former salary.

One night I was sitting on the bed, crying over an employment application form I was considering filling out when Paul came in. He sat down by my side and said, "I never asked you to go back to work." We talked about it and realized that the Lord had done his part when he sent our children. Now it was time for us to do ours. We could not break the covenant.

Finally, out of anger and frustration, I said to myself, "Fine. It's out of my hands." I decided not to worry about it anymore. I'd just stay home and be a mother.

Depression set in. In desperation I went to a women's conference. We had to choose which workshops to attend. I thought, "What if I'm in the wrong one?" Sister Karen Kinnersley spoke on a change of heart. She related it to her husband's heart transplant. She said, "You can't just take out a piece of it and expect to get better. You have to replace the whole heart." I'd never thought about that before. The Lord asks so little that I was always perfectly happy to do all he asked, but for my spare time I had big plans. I wanted to be an important person, a worldly success. This was my answer. I had been holding back a piece of my heart. A change of heart was in order.

I decided to take my problems to the only Person who could possibly help. I would have a couple of hours to myself (an unusual circumstance for a mother), and I decided to do what Enos did because I wanted to know the way Enos knew. I planned it all out. I fasted beforehand, and as you can well imagine, it is a trick for a mother to fast successfully without anyone noticing. I had a meeting that took me out of the house at dinnertime. In the morning no one ever has time to notice who eats what in the mad dash to get out the door. I didn't want anyone to know what I was going to do or how important it was to me.

When I was alone, I prayed as I had never prayed before. I said "Father, I'm finished. I can't find the answer. Nothing works. Please help me. Please tell me what to do. I have tried these many years to find my own way. Thou hast taught me many great and valuable lessons and given me many wonderful talents but to what purpose?"

Then I realized what I was saying and exactly who I was making these demands of. I began to sob. "I'm sorry, Father. Please forgive my selfish pride. I don't need to know anymore. I don't need to be in control. I am yours. My whole life I give to Thee unconditionally. I'll do anything you ask. I'll scrub floors. Do genealogy. I'll even be a Cub Scout den mother. But please, Lord, one request. (Not to be confused with conditions or demands.) Help me to make a difference. Please don't let me end up ordinary. Please help me to touch the hearts of my brothers and sisters so that when I go home to Thee, I won't go home alone. Dear Lord, what wouldst Thou have me do?"

I had never felt anything as strongly as I felt the Spirit of my Savior that day. I knew that he loved me. I knew that I was of royal birth and infinitely prized by him and by my Father in Heaven. I knew I could do whatever he asked of me because I knew I was not alone. I never had been. I never would be.

Then, just as it says in Enos 1:15, "Whatsoever thing ye shall ask in faith, believing that ye shall receive in the name of Christ, ye shall receive it," I received peace. I put my life in his hands, and he has not failed me. The miracles have poured forth from heaven faster than I can receive them. All has been restored and then some. I have also done all the things I told him I would do—the things that were my greatest fears: genealogy, Cub Scouts, and yes, even scrubbing floors. I have done them and loved the doing of them for I can never pay him back no matter how hard I try.

He has taught me how to walk in faith, one step at a time.

I cannot thank him enough. "I say unto you, my brethren, that if [I] should render all the thanks and praise which [my] whole soul has power to possess, to that God who has created [me], and has kept and preserved [me], and has caused that [I] should rejoice, and has granted that [I] should live in peace. . . .

"I say unto you that if [I] should serve him who has created [me] from the beginning, and is preserving [me] from day to day, by lending [me] breath, that [I] may live and move and do according to [my] own will, and even supporting [me] from one moment to another—I say, if [I] should serve him with all [my] whole [soul] yet [I] would be [an unprofitable servant]" (Mosiah 2:20–21).

The miracles just keep coming. There have been many challenges, but there will never be anything I can't handle, for I know from whence cometh my strength (Psalm 121:1).

I testify that there is one Father, there is one Son, there is one Holy Ghost. There is one you. There is one me. Together we will make it home. "But I have prayed for thee, that thy faith fail not: and when thou art converted, strengthen thy brethren" (Luke 22:32).

Peace comes through giving. I give you these things in the name of Jesus Christ, amen.

Diana J. Kennard is a homemaker and an artist and songwriter. She and her husband, Paul R. Kennard, perform their music and display the artwork that have come as a direct result of the change of heart spoken of in this article. She serves as stake Primary president.

Searching for Peace

VICKI RAE BLANCH

I have always believed that fasting, prayer, and scripture study are integral parts of living the gospel. For me, the fasting and prayer part has been easy, but the scripture study has been difficult.

First, I was a busy student. Then I was a very busy student and wife; then I was a very, very busy wife and teacher; then I was a very, very, very busy wife and mother. I always planned to start studying after the babies got out of diapers. Then it became when the kids were in school. Soon it was when things settle down a bit during the summer. Then it was back to when the kids were in school. I was PTA president, a school board committee member, county chairman for the cancer drive, ward chairman for the March of Dimes, state president of the dental auxiliary, a member of literary clubs, stake Young Women president—and the list goes on. I actually believed I was too busy to study the scriptures. In fact, I was too busy to do several of the things I knew I should be doing. And I was becoming more and more frustrated and unhappy.

Though I was anxiously engaged in a hundred good causes, there were a thousand other things I wasn't getting done. I wasn't experiencing feelings of achievement or success, even though I was accomplishing many good things, and I certainly wasn't experiencing peace.

For several months I struggled with feelings of inadequacy and guilt about not being worthy enough. As those feelings grew, they spilled over into every aspect of my life—mothering, "wifeing," even serving the Lord. I seemed to be treading water in the thick, dark sea of worldly demands, and I was about to go down for the last time.

I don't know exactly why I said yes when a friend asked if I'd like to take an institute class with her. After all, it would be one more demand, one more thing to take time from my already too-short day. Maybe it was because the class was called "Personal Growth and Development," and "unworthy, inadequate" me surely needed that. Maybe it was because graduating from institute was on my long list of unachieved goals.

As I started to read the scriptures for my homework assignments (I always did what I was expected to do), I found bits of wisdom here and there that fitted together like the pieces of a carefully designed puzzle. As each new piece was added, it helped me see a bigger portion of the picture.

Through prayer and study I began to understand and even to accept that I never will be able to do it all, that I never will be even close to perfect, but that "after all [I] can do" the Savior will make up the difference through his grace and his atonement (2 Nephi 25:23). "My grace is sufficient for all men that humble themselves before me; for if they humble themselves before me, and have faith in me, then will I make weak things become strong unto them" (Ether 12:27). I began to realize that my frustration and despair at being unable to accomplish all things was, in essence, a lack of understanding of the Atonement.

Through our class discussions and other studying those discussions led me to do, I have finally found peace in the knowledge that I don't have to do it all myself. The Lord will pick up the slack. He will accept my efforts and sacrifices and make "weak things become strong unto [me]." What I need to do is quit running so fast in the world and turn my direction toward the Lord. I need to quit trying to do all things and concentrate on the few things that are going to make all the difference, particularly, my own spirituality and my relationship with the Savior.

I finally understand that I don't have to run faster than I can, that it's okay to seek calm and peace and order, that I don't have to be everything to everybody as long as I'm building closer relationships with my Heavenly Father and my family. Although this notion is foreign to my earthly mind, it feels very true to my soul. In pondering this concept, I have realized that the Spirit has been trying to bear witness to me of this principle for at least seven or eight years. But until my institute class, I had not slowed down long enough to recognize his promptings.

I am beginning to realize that, like Old Mother Hubbard, I must stock my cupboards before I can be valiant in my service to others and to the Lord. I must take time to fill my mind with good thoughts, music, and understanding, rather than run so fast plowing that I forget to let the flowers grow.

I've come to understand that my great weakness is trying to be too strong. I must learn to lean on the Lord, trust him in all things, and accept his gift of grace.

Another unexpected blessing has also come into my life: I've found my days are longer. I am able to study the scriptures and still complete most of the things on my list! I have never been able to accomplish most of the things on my list, let alone study, too, so this is a huge change. I've been told that I have just learned to prioritize better so my lists are shorter, but I truly believe that my hours have been lengthened and my days have been stretched.

I look forward to getting my work in the world finished so I can get to my scripture study. I've come to realize what it means to thirst for knowledge, "feast upon the words of Christ," and "[delight] in the scriptures" (2 Nephi 9:50; 32:3; 4:15).

I've discovered that whatever problem I have or question I'm pondering, the answers and insights are right there in the scriptures. And every time I read—even if I've read the same passage before—I find something new. The books remain the same, but I do not. Every day my experiences change and make me grow, and every day my study awakens new understanding.

That institute class and the scripture study that it encouraged were truly answers to my prayers. They have helped me figure out who I really am and who the Lord wants me to be. That has motivated me to change my focus and improve my life. It has also caused me to have a renewed understanding of his special love for me as distinct from the general love he feels for all of his children. My faith has increased, and as it says in Alma 5:12, "according to [this] faith there was a mighty change wrought in [my] heart."

I am learning when to say yes and how to say no. I am discovering that I don't have to please everyone to be able to please the Lord. I have even found time to graduate from institute. Perhaps the reason I was feeling so overwhelmed was that I was too engaged in worldly causes, albeit good causes, rather than the work of God. "Remember, remember that it is not the work of God that is frustrat[ing], but the work of men" (D&C 3:3).

My guilt is steadily being replaced with the peace that comes from knowing that "his hand is stretched out still" (2 Nephi 19:12), despite my inadequacies, and that I can be "encircled about eternally in the arms of his love" (2 Nephi 1:15). After all is said and done, that is what really matters.

Vicki Rae Eyre Blanch has taught high school English and worked as a teacher's assistant in an applied technology center. Now a full-time homemaker, she and her husband, Joe, are the parents of six children. She served for many years in Young Women and currently teaches in her ward Relief Society.

Finding Peace

SUSAN M. PROBST

For the past year my focus had been on the completion of a new home in Heber Valley. We had been prayerful in this decision and felt strongly that this was what we should do. It seemed that all we had worked for had finally paid off and we would now live the perfect life in the perfect home.

We believed we had the abilities and talents to complete much of the work on the home ourselves, which we set out to do. At the end of nine months, exhausted, with a home that was ninety-five percent finished, I found myself becoming distraught over the flaws in the construction of our new home. Because we were the ones who had done the work, I was acutely aware of every little glitch. These imperfections were mostly inconsequential, ranging from tiny paint drips to cracks in tile to not-quite-perfect color choices, but I let them eat at me. We had also put ourselves in a financial bind, and the pressure we were under seemed insurmountable.

I found myself unable to focus on anything but the negatives. My expectations of the perfect life had gone down the drain, and I surrendered to despair and gloom, a state I have since come to recognize as depression. For the next six months, I sat on my front porch and felt sorry for myself, becoming increasingly drained physically, mentally, and spiritually. I had gone through other experiences that were more trying and difficult, but this time I let unrealistic expectations overcome me. I didn't know what to do or where to turn. I prayed for peace, but my thoughts remained focused on everything that had gone wrong. When my prayers didn't seem to help, I began desiring a visit, or a dream, or something more tangible to get me out of this despondency. I wanted someone to come tell me that I was okay, that the decisions I had made were okay, and that things would get better.

One week in Sunday School we were discussing that very thing. I raised my hand and said I desired a vision. A dear woman in our ward looked me straight in the eye and said, "You are just feeling lonely. People are watching out for you. The veil is thin. Heavenly Father is aware of you." I felt her spirit. I believed what she said.

While preparing a Young Women lesson not long afterward, I came upon this quotation from President Joseph Fielding Smith: "When a man has the manifestation from the Holy Ghost, it leaves an indelible impression on his soul, one that is not easily erased. It is Spirit speaking to spirit, and it comes with convincing force. A manifestation of an angel, or even of the Son of God himself, would impress the eye and mind, and eventually become dimmed, but the impressions of the Holy Ghost sink deeper into the soul and are more difficult to erase." (*Answers to Gospel Questions* [Salt Lake City: Deseret Book, 1958], 2:151.) He also stated that "through the Holy Ghost the truth is woven into the very fibre and sinews of the body so that it cannot be forgotten" (*Doctrines of Salvation* [Salt Lake City, Bookcraft, 1954], 1:48). Reading those statements put to rest my desire for a heavenly visitor. I had felt the Spirit before and knew the strength that comes from such an experience. It was clear to me that I needed to make the effort to figure things out for myself, knowing that Heavenly Father would bless me in that endeavor.

In December I attended the Relief Society Christmas dinner. The program featured a woman in our ward who had gone through some hard times and had finally decided to allow Heavenly Father to direct her life. She had knelt down and said, "Father, I will do whatever you desire of me." I had based many of my adult decisions on the theme "I will follow God's plan for me," so I knew what she was talking about, but I needed to do that again with greater fervor.

The first of the year brought an overnight visit from my parents. I had been experiencing severe heartburn and was wondering if I had an ulcer. Besides all the emotional and spiritual turmoil I was feeling, we were now not sure how we were going to pay the mortgage. I didn't want to share any of this with my parents, nor did I want financial help from them. The next morning, over breakfast, my father said that he had awakened during the night with the thought that we needed money. Tears welled up in my eyes. I told him of our concerns, and he pulled out his checkbook to make us a loan. I felt that Heavenly Father had blessed me that day through my father. I realized the significance of their visit. Now that the wall was down, my father wondered aloud if I weren't a bit depressed. Looking back, I recognize that I was, but that day, for the first time in six months, I began to feel that things were going to be all right.

That day brought with it the thought that I needed to find peace in who I was. If I could find this inner peace, then what went on around me and the imperfections of tangible things probably wouldn't matter. Thus I found my own theme for 1995: "Finding Peace."

Luckily for me, the theme of the Young Women for that year was "Feasting upon the Word." The goal in our ward was to read the Book of Mormon in ninety days, and I accepted the challenge. The words came alive to me. I grasped their meaning, and this time as I read two things struck me. The first was what I read in Ether 12:27: "And if men come unto me I will show unto them their weakness. I give unto men weakness that they may be humble; and my grace is sufficient for all men that humble themselves before me; for if they humble themselves before me, and have faith in me, then will I make weak things become strong unto them." Reading this scripture made me feel that if I asked for help in finding peace, I would be blessed with peace.

The other thing I noticed with renewed force was the problems that people of the Book of Mormon encountered when they "set their hearts upon the vain things of the world" (Helaman 12:4). I began letting go of some of the materialistic desires I had been carrying around with me for a long time. I realized that not only had I been carrying around very worldly desires but other vanities as well: grudges, jealousies, perfectionistic expectations, and so forth. I determined I needed to rid myself of that excess baggage.

Things began to improve. I was feeling better about myself because I was reading the scriptures, praying, and had received priesthood blessings from my husband. Then several frustrating things happened that finally built up to a flood of tears and the desperate need to pray out loud for help from my Heavenly Father. This time the prayer wasn't just "please help me to find peace" but such specific things as "I don't feel that this is fair because . . ." and "It just doesn't seem right that . . ." An interesting thing happened as I continued praying. Thoughts began coming into my mind, such as "Please forgive me for . . ." and "Please let me be aware of . . ." The next flood of thoughts began with "I am so thankful for . . ." When I opened my eyes, I remembered that I was all alone, but I didn't feel that way. The excess baggage was gone. The negative thoughts and opinions I had been carrying around for years were gone. The atonement of the Savior had new meaning to me. I felt peace.

This peace empowered me for the next several months. Things didn't bother me as much as they had in the past. I had a new perspective of who I was. I truly began to believe I was a daughter of God and I had much to do on this earth. I spent time reading good books, listening to uplifting music, and thinking more positive thoughts. I had learned that when we base our self-esteem on anything other than the knowledge that we are daughters of our Heavenly Father, we will have short spurts of peace followed by increased confusion, frustration, and depression. I now recognized that the only way to have true peace is to gain this knowledge of who we truly are and to put our trust in our Heavenly Father, not in the things of the world.

In November my family visited my parents in Kirtland, Ohio. On Thanksgiving night, my parents took us on a tour of the Newell K. Whitney store. I was excited to see the store, and I looked forward to hearing of the history that took place there. I was not expecting the information I was told in the upper room of the store called the "School of the Prophets." The first high priests of the Church were being taught there by Joseph Smith when the Father and the Son appeared to them. As I sat there, I felt as if I were being held in someone's arms. I knew what was being said was true. The chorus of a children's hymn kept running through my mind:

> He knows I will follow him,
> Give all my life to him.
> I feel my Savior's love,
> The love he freely gives me.
>
> Children's Songbook (Salt Lake City: The Church of Jesus
> Christ of Latter-day Saints, 1989), 74

It was the final chapter of my year of finding peace.

Susan M. Probst is a homemaker. She and her husband, Kimball W. Probst, have one son. She serves as Primary president in her ward.

FINDING PEACE
THROUGH ACKNOWLEDGING THE
ATONEMENT OF CHRIST

Balm of Gilead

RUTH M. WORKMAN

There it was—at the very bottom of the plastic carton way back on the shelf of the hall linen closet—a small, round, red, metal container about the size of a fifty-cent piece with Tiger Balm spelled out in ornate lettering on the lid. I had forgotten all about it and even why I had purchased it, except that as I felt the cool metal in the hollow of my hand, I remembered I had been on a trip to the coast and spotted the cardboard tiger display at the back of a store. It was the bright red that drew my interest, I guess. I always did love red. It was my only purchase, and at the time, I threw the tin into my purse, only to find it there days later.

The first time I opened the tin, the aroma of menthol filled the room, and I got a cool-and-then-warm sensation when I rubbed a little of the balm on the inside of my wrist. But after a while the little red tin found its way to the top of the medicine cabinet and finally to the back of the top shelf of the hall closet. This one is definitely a keeper! I think, and I toss the little tin onto the biggest pile as I continue to dig my way through the mess in the closet. Three piles, growing by the minute, are blocking the hall. One is the "keeper" pile, one the "definitely toss" pile, and the third a "think about it later" pile. I am beginning to realize that I had taken on too big a challenge for a winter afternoon, or perhaps I had started it too late in the day. Whatever the reason, I can't stop now; I can't turn back.

Earlier that day I had been going over the ward's homemaking lessons for the coming year and, as the Home Management teacher, thought it would be a good idea to familiarize myself with the next topic. "An Orderly Home"—how appropriate! I had definitely been planning for months to get things in order, and so now, on this dreary, rainy, winter day I find myself cleaning out closets, sorting through the accumulation of years, and making piles on the floor. But my eye keeps returning to the bright red of the tin, and my mind remembers the soothing comfort of the herbal scent from the salve inside. I try to twist the lid open to see what's left, but try as I might, I can't get it open. It appears to be stuck. I ask my seventeen-year-old son to give me a hand, but he, too, becomes frustrated after a few tries and says, "Give it up, Mom. It's glued shut. Just throw it away!" Finally, I leave everything—the piles in the hall, the mess in the closet—and take the tin out to the garage, place it in a vise on the workbench, and with a pair of pliers pry open the lid. Ah! There is the mild, refreshing fragrance I have been remembering. I take in long, deep breaths and savor the moment. I suddenly begin to remember that trip to the coast: the friends who were with me, the joy and sincerity of true friendship that continues as we grow older, the beauty of the California coastline at sunset, the enjoyment of simple pleasures. I weep unashamed there in the garage as I ponder the love I am feeling in my heart.

And then it comes to me! These same feelings of joy and love are what I receive when I participate in my calling in Relief Society. The calm and soothing emotions I experience are not the result of an herbal aroma but of the shared sisterhood we have in the gospel of Jesus Christ. In the dignity of service comes the true rest I long to have. I remember how comforted I felt when, at a recent family preparedness homemaking night, I found my family's name on the ward's emergency/disaster list along with the name of the elder who would contact me in case of emergency. Because my husband is a policeman and would be among the first to be called out in a disaster, to know that someone would check on me and my family left me with such a feeling of peace and contentment that tears flow again as I remember that wonderful evening.

I ponder the strength I feel when researching my lessons,

preparing to visit a sister in need, or working on a special assistance program or Christmas project. I am reminded of the truthfulness of the Church and all that has been set down for us to read and study. There, in itself, is the true balm. It is not in that little red container from the back of the closet shelf but in the holy scriptures, patiently waiting for me to pry them open and partake of the healing, comforting words inside. The patient love of the Father, so beautifully told in those pages, is the salve for my wounds. The blessed story of the Savior is the ointment for any hurt. The outline of how we should live our lives, the decrees of the commandments, and the power of the plan of salvation—that is the emollient for my soul.

Slowly I dry my eyes, close the lid on the tiny tin, and decide to hurry back inside to finish my tasks. But first I will sit for a peaceful moment to enjoy the true balm—to read a passage or two from those beautiful, blessed words of the scriptures and feel the quiet peace that comes only from the Savior, the true Balm of Gilead.

Ruth M. Workman is a part-time secretary and a resource parent for families of special-education students. She and her husband are the parents of three sons. She serves as home management leader in her ward Relief Society.

Balm for Adversity

KAREN BAKER

Thomas J. kicked a beehive as he shuffled through layers of dead leaves. His friend, Vada, had lost a treasured ring on a hike here in the woods, and Thomas J. was intent on finding it. He didn't realize he had disturbed a nest of bees until they were angrily swarming around him. He tried to fend them off with his arms, but there were too many of them. One bee after another stung Thomas J., and in a few moments he collapsed. He was allergic to bee stings, and this attack was fatal.

Like Thomas J. in the movie *My Girl*, each of us is vulnerable to the stings of adversity. No one is immune, even those engaged in doing good deeds; however, there is an antidote for the poison of adversity. The balm of Gilead soothes and detoxifies the sorrows of this life so that they cannot injure us permanently. Carlfred Broderick has said: "The gospel of Jesus Christ is not insurance against pain. It is resource in event of pain, and when that pain comes . . . rejoice that you have resource to deal with your pain" ("The Uses of Adversity," in *As Women of Faith*, ed. Mary E. Stovall and Carol Cornwall Madsen [Salt Lake City: Deseret Book, 1989], 172–73).

The gospel of Jesus Christ conveys peace to our hearts through the gift of the Holy Ghost. By doing "the works of righteousness" it will give us "peace in this world" while preparing us for "eternal life in the world to come" (D&C 59:23).

Like many others, I attended Brigham Young University, where I met a returned missionary whose father was a bishop. We were married in the temple, had four children, and prospered financially. We served in various leadership and teaching capacities in the ward and stake. People commented that we were a perfect family. But we were not. There was another side to our life. My husband was abusive to our children and to me.

Unfortunately, my experiences are not unique. Probably everyone knows someone who has been abused. After years of struggle, counseling, and prayer, I decided to seek a divorce. I sought the support of a new bishop who didn't know me, and I approached the interview unsure of the reception I would receive. He reminded me of the difficulties of rearing children alone. I agreed that it seemed a challenging prospect at best. He opened his scriptures and read Doctrine and Covenants 6:23: "Did I not speak peace to your mind concerning the matter? What greater witness can you have than from God?" He paused and asked, "Do you have such a witness?" I answered, "That is the only thing I do have." My bishop simply replied, "I will help you in any way I can." I later received a blessing from my stake president that twice confirmed that I had made the correct decision for my family. He added that in the premortal life I had chosen this burden, knowing the growth I would experience.

I cannot adequately express the pain or the difficulties my children and I have dealt with as a result of the divorce. Moreover, I could not at first understand how my children could be healed from the effects of the abuse they had suffered. The destructive behavior patterns were extreme and deeply rooted. And though everything possible was being done to help my children heal, all our efforts were insufficient. I knew the Lord wiped away the sin from the lives of sinners, but my children were innocent victims who still suffered the effects of sin. Who would cover that?

Yet I was blessed with a feeling of peace. The influence of the Holy Ghost affirmed that the Lord knew our plight and loved us. I found that only through the Atonement could I have hope. I learned firsthand that the Lord can give "beauty for ashes" (Isaiah 61:3). Through study, prayer, temple attendance, and the support of dear friends in the gospel, I have come to understand the power of the Atonement to heal all the hurts that we suffer, whether they are due to our own sins or the sins of others. I have learned that "along with such gifts as hope and charity, these blessings [of the Atonement] include the healing of spiritual wounds and compensation for spiritual losses. As we continue to do 'all we can do' (2 Nephi 25:23) on our own power, the Savior closes the remaining gaps" (Bruce C. Hafen and Marie K. Hafen, *The Belonging Heart* [Salt Lake City: Deseret Book, 1994], 121).

How can any of us hope to qualify for the compensatory blessings of the Atonement? Elder Dean L. Larsen has stated: "It has seemed to me that built into the conscience of every human soul is the most accurate determiner of whether we are living in such a way as to merit the ultimate blessings promised to the faithful. We point to this determiner when we say, 'Be honest with yourself.' A person does not easily deceive his own conscience. Deep within our own hearts we generally know when we have paid the price, when we have done the best our personal resources and abilities would have allowed us to do at the moment, regardless of the outcome of our effort or the way it may be viewed by others. It is at these times that we know real peace, even though the product of our effort may not be all that we would have hoped it to be" ("The Peaceable Things of the Kingdom," in *Hope* [Salt Lake City: Deseret Book, 1988], 200–201).

Thus, peace may be obtained in part by developing spiritual maturity. The influence of the Spirit then secures our hope of eternal life. Those who place their hope in the Savior know that his atonement balances all unequal earthly equations, and that the Lord has his own perfect timetable and scales. Some blessings that the Lord has in mind for us may not come until we pass from this life. Yet we can always have hope for ourselves and those we love, knowing that the Lord can make a blessing out of any trial.

To avail ourselves of such blessings it is necessary to exhibit trust in him by exerting patience. Elder Neal A. Maxwell has wisely said:

"Patience is not indifference. Actually, it is caring very much, but being willing, nevertheless, to submit both to the Lord and to what the scriptures call the 'process of time.' . . .

"In our approach to life, patience also helps us to realize that while we may be ready to move on, having had enough of a particular learning experience, our continuing presence is often a needed part of the learning environment of others. Patience is thus closely connected with two other central attributes of Christianity—love and humility. . . .

"Since our competition in life, as Elder Boyd K. Packer of the Quorum of the Twelve has perceptively said, is solely with our old self, we ought to be free of the jealousies and anxieties of the world which go with interpersonal competition. Very importantly, it is patience, combined with love, which permits us 'in process of time' to detoxify our disappointments. Patience and love take the radioactivity out of our resentments. These are neither small nor occasional needs in most of our lives! . . .

"Clearly, patience so cradles us amidst suffering. Paul, who had suffered much, observed in his epistle to the Hebrews: 'Now no chastening for the present seemeth to be joyous, but grievous: nevertheless afterward it yieldeth the peaceable fruit of righteousness unto them which are exercised thereby' ([Hebrews] 12:11)" ("Patience," *Ensign*, Oct. 1980, 28–29).

One of the peaceable fruits of righteousness is forgiveness. Though we may sometimes think of forgiveness as a duty, a difficulty, or an obligation, forgiveness is, in fact, a blessing. Forgiveness, like faith, is a positive force that prevents us from being distracted by recrimination. "It is a sin not to forgive, because sin is defined as that which impedes spiritual growth and happiness—in this case, our own. . . . It is simply in our best interests to forgive.

"The more we have been hurt, the more we deserve to forgive" (Wendy L. Ulrich, "When Forgiveness Flounders: For Victims of Serious Sin," *Confronting Abuse*, ed. Anne Horton, B. Kent Harrison, and Barry L. Johnson [Salt Lake City: Deseret Book, 1993], 348).

Our efforts to forgive connect us to the ultimate source of

healing and peace. "The Atonement infuses into our lives other blessings of the Savior's grace, endowing us with affirmative gifts that fill our souls with hope, charity, and, ultimately, all of the perfecting attributes of a divine nature, which is what it means to have eternal (godlike) life" (Hafen and Hafen, *Belonging Heart*, 152).

President Heber J. Grant wrote: "I do not believe that any man lives up to his ideals, but if we are striving, if we are working, if we are trying, to the best of our ability, to improve day by day, then we are in the line of our duty. If we are seeking to remedy our own defects, if we are so living that we can ask God for light, for knowledge, for intelligence, and above all, for His Spirit, that we may overcome our weaknesses, then, I can tell you, we are in the straight and narrow path that leads to life eternal. Then we need have no fear" (*Gospel Standards*, comp. G. Homer Durham [Salt Lake City: Improvement Era, 1969], 184–85).

Eternal life is what the Lord wants for all of us. He wants to free us from fear so that we may experience the gift of peace in our lives. He wants us to be with him in eternity. We do our part by striving to stay close to our Father in Heaven and obeying his commandments. He will bless us with peace through the companionship of the Holy Ghost and secure our hope in the eternal life to come through the atonement of our Savior, Jesus Christ, the one true Balm of Gilead.

Karen M. Baker was married to John M. Baker Jr. in 1989, and they have six children: one each in college, high school, junior high, elementary school, and preschool, and one still at home. She earned her bachelor's degree from the University of California–Irvine in 1993. She teaches in her ward Relief Society.

"Is There No Balm in Gilead?"

JANIEL REEVE CARVER

During times of deepest trial, I have looked into the heavens as if trying to part the veil to see or hear answers to my fervent prayers. I have often wondered during those times why the heavens seemed closed to me, and I have asked with the prophet Jeremiah, "Is there no balm in Gilead?" (8:22). It has taken many years to realize that the Lord answers prayers according to his own timetable. Sometimes he lets us suffer heartache to strengthen and shape our character and to teach us to walk by faith. If he were to intervene immediately when we pray for relief, there would be no stretching or growing. There would be no test. For our own good, he does not offer us immediate surcease of our trials.

Elder Bruce R. McConkie wrote: "It is not, never has been, and never will be the design and purpose of the Lord—however much we seek him in prayer—to answer all our problems and concerns without struggle and effort on our part. This mortality is a probationary estate. . . . We are being tested to see how we will respond in various situations; how we will decide issues; what course we will pursue while we are here walking, not by sight, but by faith" ("Why the Lord Ordained Prayer," *Ensign*, Jan. 1976, 11).

What he does offer us is balm through the comfort of the Holy Ghost and through the atonement of the Savior, which, if used, will bind up every wound and make our adversity "but a small moment" (D&C 121:7) even if our trial encompasses years of our lives. So it was to be with me. One night, at age fourteen, I

135

lay in bed and prayed with all the strength of my faith for my Heavenly Father to remove the cup he had given me. I felt, as Joseph Smith felt in Liberty Jail, that I had been enclosed in the walls of a prison without cause.

From the time I was eight, I found myself a victim of the effects of my father's alcoholism. My two oldest siblings had left home by then, and only my next-older brother and I remained. Through years of drunken rages, disappearances, drunk driving arrests, and abuse, I withdrew into my own world. I knew that the Lord would not give me more than I was able to bear, but I felt that I could bear no more. As I lay in bed that night in my fourteenth year, I told my Father in Heaven that I could no longer live under those conditions and pleaded with him to remove the burden from me. I prayed that my father would stop drinking and restore our family life.

There was no immediate answer, no balm for my troubled heart. "My God, my God, why hast thou forsaken me? why art thou so far from helping me, and from the words of my roaring? O my God, I cry in the daytime, but thou hearest not; and in the night season, and am not silent" (Psalm 22:1–2). The gospel seemed to hold no solace for me because there came no relief from the trial through heartfelt prayer. I was too young then to realize the comfort and help I received from the Holy Ghost through each individual trial as I tried to cope with my life.

My prayer did not seem to be answered until I had graduated from college, married, and moved to another state. My uncle called me at that time to say that he was praying not for my dad to quit drinking but for him to hit bottom and be driven to his knees. He felt that only being totally humbled by the Lord would turn my father from his iniquity.

I cried to think that he would pray for such a thing and hoped that his prayers would not be answered. Within days, however, my uncle's plea to the Lord came to pass. My mother left my father, filed for divorce, and had to be secretly removed from the state to live with me when he became violent. He then suffered a massive stroke and was totally paralyzed, without speech and near death. When the call came that he was in the hospital, my mother said to me, "I would never forgive myself if after forty years of marriage, I didn't go back to care for him and he died." Dad had been inactive in the Church for most of his married life, had caused our family to suffer and be torn apart, and had been disciplined by a Church disciplinary counsel. Yet we all loved him.

My mother and I flew to Utah. By the time we got there, Dad had been transported from our small hometown to Provo, and we followed him there. He had brain surgery to remove a subdural hematoma but afterward still suffered from the effects of the stroke. My family was distraught, afraid that he would die and yet afraid of what would happen if he didn't. My sister, who had flown home from New York to be at his bedside, said, "Don't pray for strength for me. I don't want any more trials."

After a few days, with our family all gathered at the hospital, I seemed to be the only one who could understand the few words my father could utter. He was restless and uneasy and seemed to be asking for my mother, who had not yet been in to see him. I went out of his hospital room and told Mom that he was asking for her. She went to him. He immediately became calm and was able to start healing.

What happened from that point on was nothing short of miraculous. The stroke had damaged the speech and conscious-thought center of his brain, and he was paralyzed. Yet he was able to regain total movement and learn to speak and think clearly. Even his memory returned. For a month my mother and I stayed with him in the hospital to help nurse him until he was finally able to go home. What had changed was his personality. With that change came the ability to overcome the effects of alcoholism. From that time on, he never drank, and finally, after forty years, he started to go to church again.

I spent the next several months at home with my parents to help with the recovery. I was able to witness them forgiving each other and forging a new marriage out of the ashes of the old. Finally, an answer to my prayer. It had taken ten years for the answer to come—years of misery, heartache, and pain that would forever affect the lives of our family members.

Dad became active in the Church and eventually became worthy to go the temple. He and my mother served a three-year mission as ordinance workers in the Manti Temple. The peace and joy they found in that assignment healed years of pain. Their relationship became a celestial one as they served together in the house of the Lord.

There were many trials yet to come. My father was diagnosed with cancer of the throat from the many years of alcohol abuse and had to have the side of his neck and throat removed. He was restricted to a liquid diet and suffered through radiation treatments. My mother had three major surgeries over the next ten years and was diagnosed with Parkinson's disease. Even so, those ten years were the happiest our family had ever known, and Dad took care of Mom with the same dedication with which she had nursed him after his stroke. Finally, he contracted pneumonia and died within two weeks. Yet he died having repented and possessing faith in his Savior and His atoning sacrifice.

Three years later, my mother passed away. Through all the years of her life she had been active in the gospel, persevered through hardship and trial, reared her family in the gospel, and remained faithful. Her funeral was not filled with despair, for death for her was a joyous occasion. She had returned to that God who gave her life to receive the reward of a daughter who had remained faithful and endured every trial to the end of her mortal life.

My heart was drawn to a scripture in the Doctrine and Covenants: "For verily I say unto you, blessed is he that keepeth my commandments, whether in life or in death; and he that is faithful in tribulation, the reward of the same is greater in the kingdom of heaven. Ye cannot behold with your natural eyes, for the present time, the design of your God concerning those things which shall come hereafter, and the glory which shall follow after much tribulation. For after much tribulation come the blessings.

Wherefore the day cometh that ye shall be crowned with much glory" (D&C 58:2–4).

Little did I know that those early trials would later precipitate my own. All the children in my parents' family have suffered the effects of having an alcoholic parent. Among those effects are judging oneself without mercy, difficulty having fun or finding joy in life, difficulty with intimate relationships, pervasive anger, codependency, being controlling, being unable to say no because of what others might think, perfectionism, low tolerance of frustration, avoidance of conflict, depression, low self-esteem, perpetual fear of the unknown, repression of feelings, trying to be a people pleaser, obsessive/compulsive behavior, feeling wounded, and feeling over-responsible. The most damaging of these effects is a pervasive sense of inadequacy and unworthiness regardless of their having done nothing to bring these feelings upon themselves. The sin is not theirs, yet many children of alcoholics grow up feeling that the Atonement applies to everyone except them and that even the Savior's sacrifice is not enough to save them from the shame, guilt, and torment they feel.

These axioms, internalized as a child, remain and define relationships with spouse and children in later years. At age thirty-five, when I had hoped to have put my past life completely behind me, I faced the biggest trial I had yet faced. I found that I could not overcome the effects of my father's alcoholism without help. I was suffering from having been reared in this lifestyle, and it was affecting my own family relationships. I have a daughter so much like me that we could be twins thirty years apart. I saw myself treating her the same way I had been treated as a child, even though I was not an alcoholic. That realization was devastating to me.

The adult child of an alcoholic (ACA) has no coping mechanism to withstand the natural shocks that normal childhood behavior administers to parents. ACAs have developed deep wells of anger from what happened to them. Their anger is channeled into critical attitudes toward self and others. They bring a hypersensitive perception of responsibility to adulthood. Once they become parents, that hypersensitive perception can be too much to bear, and when the anger breaks out, their children are the targets. When ACAs leave their childhood home, they feel they have left behind the effects of an alcoholic home. They can marry and develop a relationship, but when children come, the emotional equilibrium is upset and symptoms of the disease surface. ACAs find themselves still controlled by the behavior and needs of their alcoholic parent. That leads to the need to control their own lives as adults and the need to control the behavior of their children. It becomes a vicious cycle not compatible with gospel standards and principles. Christlike love is not a factor in this cycle. Recovery is a lifetime process.

I began suffering major bouts with depression and anger. In the beginning, I didn't understand what was wrong with me. Fortunately, diagnosis for me was fast in coming. Our stake had a symposium for children of alcoholics and abusers conducted by trained professionals, and I went. It changed my life. At last I knew what was wrong and was so relieved that I could fix it. Little did I know how hard that would be. There is no quick fix. It takes years of self-examination, behavioral change, and sometimes therapy to overcome the problem. I joined a Latter-day Saint ACA group and went to a therapist for six months to understand, talk, and get through the depression. I read every self-help book I could find. Getting well became my occupation. I met with my bishop for counseling and counseled with my husband, who was extremely supportive. I prayed for guidance and strength and spent hours in the scriptures seeking help. I began to wonder through all my trials if there was any peace to be found. Would there never be joy in my life?

I read in Isaiah 61:1–3: "He hath sent me to bind up the brokenhearted, to proclaim liberty to the captives, and the opening of the prison to them that are bound; . . . to comfort all that mourn; to appoint unto them that mourn in Zion, to give unto them beauty for ashes, the oil of joy for mourning, the garment of praise for the spirit of heaviness." I truly felt a captive. Could I find the relief this scripture promised?

Finally, when the pain was almost too much to bear, I fell to my knees. I pleaded with my Heavenly Father for the effects of this abuse and my guilt and suffering to be swept away. A feeling of joy, peace, forgiveness, and love came over me, and the burden was lifted from my heart. Like Alma, I felt relief from pain and the gall of bitterness. "I cried within my heart: O Jesus, thou Son of God, have mercy on me, who am in the gall of bitterness, and am encircled about by the everlasting chains of death. And now, behold, when I thought this, I could remember my pains no more" (Alma 36:18–19).

The Atonement is not just for sinners. Its effects relieve every burden that we will place before our Lord and Savior. I had to be completely humbled before I went to the Lord and asked for relief from my pain. Through the power of the Atonement, he changed my life and has allowed me to heal, to forgive, to re-parent myself and my children. It has taken ten years, but I now have peace and feel joy in my life, my marriage, and my children. I am breaking the cycle of abuse and clinging to the hope of my Savior's atonement to ease every burden. My growth has been beyond my own ability. Only with His help have I been able to find peace. "Come unto me, all ye that . . . are heavy laden, and I will give you rest. Take my yoke upon you, and learn of me; for I am meek and lowly in heart: and ye shall find rest unto your souls. For my yoke is easy, and my burden is light" (Matthew 11:28–30).

My burden has truly been made light by my Savior. He has not forgotten me. "For the Lord hath comforted his people, and will have mercy upon his afflicted. . . . yet will I not forget thee. Behold, I have graven thee upon the palms of my hands" (Isaiah 49:13, 15–16). President Gordon B. Hinckley said, "To call upon the Lord for wisdom beyond our own, for strength to do what we ought to do, for comfort and consolation, and for the expression of gratitude is a significant and wonderful thing" (*Ensign*, Nov. 1995, 89).

I have learned through my experience that true peace and happiness come by keeping the commandments in total obedience; putting my trust in the Lord, looking to God to live, and giving my will over to the Father, knowing that he has a plan for me and is all-knowing and infinite; coming to know that he loves me individually and is mindful of my adversity; developing a personal relationship with my Savior, who descended below us all to die that we might live; forgiving those who have wronged me; praying earnestly and living righteously to acquire the comfort, guidance, and peace of the Holy Ghost; making and keeping sacred covenants that lead to salvation; offering charity to others to take my mind from my own sorrows. I have learned to be patient in my afflictions and trust in the Lord: "Be patient in afflictions, for thou shalt have many; but endure them, for, lo, I am with thee, even unto the end of thy days" (D&C 24:8). I have learned that there is indeed a Balm in Gilead:

> *Is there no balm in Gilead?*
> *Is there no peace to be found?*
> *No balm for your soul,*
> *To make your life whole,*
> *No lasting joy to abound?*
>
> *Is there no balm in Gilead?*
> *Is there no answer to prayers?*
> *No trust in the Lord,*
> *No hope in His word,*
> *No evidence that He cares?*
>
> *Yes, there is balm in Gilead.*
> *Yes, there is cause for relief.*
> *If we learn how to give,*
> *He will teach us to live*
> *With the pain, heartache, and grief.*
>
> *By repentance, patience, trust, and love,*
> *With faith, our hearts will be filled.*
> *If we have the hope,*
> *The patience to cope,*
> *The calamities of life can be stilled.*

"Is There No Balm in Gilead?"

Peace comes by the still small voice,
By obedience and faith in the Lord.
He gives us his peace,
Our heartaches will cease,
If we learn to trust in his word.

Yes, there is Balm in Gilead!
Each sister can find his peace.
Know of his love,
Seek help from above,
Your faith in him will increase.

© Janiel Reeve Carver

Janiel Reeve Carver is a homemaker and a community volunteer. She has served as Relief Society president in her ward and is now a temple preparation class teacher and Achievement Day leader. She enjoys writing poetry and creating programs and productions for her ward and stake. She and her husband, Paul S. Carver, have three daughters.

A Daughter of Christ

KATIE MARIE HANSEN

Peace was something I had searched for since childhood but had never found. I hadn't known peace, and yet I knew I could find it. So when my husband and I moved to the town where I had grown up, in the place where my agony had begun, I was torn. We moved. What else could I do? No one knew of my torment. It had been a well-kept secret all of these years.

My husband and I bought a place high on a mountaintop surrounded by three hundred acres of oaks and pines. As I walked through the leaves that fall, I knew it was time to face my yesterdays and the sadness they had brought into my life. I didn't know how I was going to accomplish that, but I knew my Heavenly Father had brought me back. I knew I could find peace nowhere else.

When I was twenty-two and joined the Church, I felt I had found that peace. When they said all my sins were forgiven, I felt I had beaten the sadness and lack of self-worth that had plagued me while I was growing up. With the birth of my second child, I realized that these negative feelings were only buried and far from being healed. It was a fast birth. I had been very sick several times during the pregnancy. I had almost miscarried once, but I begged the Lord to let me keep this child, and my prayers were answered. Shortly after being taken to my room from the delivery room, my temperature soared to 104 degrees. Afraid that I might have something contagious, the nurse yelled, "Get her out of here. She doesn't belong here." I had just delivered a baby, and the maternity ward was most assuredly where I belonged, but at that instant it seemed as if all of heaven were screaming, "No! She doesn't belong here." In my delirium, I was trying to get into the celestial kingdom, and I was not going to be allowed in. "She's not worthy. She never will be worthy. How did she think, after all she had done as a child, that she would ever be able to enter the celestial kingdom? Never! Get her out!"

I got well. The cause of my illness was a separated pubic bone and pneumonia—both of which were curable. But that delirous nightmare became my life. I begged the Lord for forgiveness and promised to work hard so that Heavenly Father would be proud of me and let me return to the celestial kingdom. I washed every dish at every social held in our ward. I volunteered for every compassionate service assignment given. I baby-sat every child who needed tending. I supported every cause known to man, and yet none of this frantic activity brought the peace I was searching for. I knew I would never be worthy to be a daughter of my Heavenly Father.

I wanted to adopt a child in addition to our own precious children. We began the process, but there was a catch: you had to be honest about your childhood. No, I couldn't do that. This was the same welfare department my mother had worked in when I was a child. Maybe some of the people there still knew my mother. No, adoption was a dream that couldn't come true. I couldn't do this. I'd never told my parents, and I didn't want them to find out now. I withdrew our names. Nonetheless, the department called a few months later and said they had a little boy they thought would fit into our family. Would we come in for the interview? I sat quietly. Could I be honest after all these years? To have this dream, I was going to have to let go of the secret. Did I have that kind of courage?

As we spoke to the interviewer, I said, "There is something you should know about my life." As I unraveled that well-kept secret, my husband was astonished to learn that his wife had been molested as a child. The sadness and guilt were all revealed. No wonder there had been some tough spots in our marriage. A lot of things made sense to him now.

Though we were unable to adopt that little boy, the opportunity to discuss doing so has proved a great blessing. In the months and years of counseling and caring that have followed, I found the child inside me who was a daughter of her Heavenly Father, and I grew to believe in the woman inside me who is a daughter of her Heavenly Father. He had always been there for me and had held me up when I had lost the strength and courage to do so myself. I grew to understand I couldn't become worthy of that honor through doing dishes, baby-sitting, or performing any other chore here on earth. We cannot work out our own salvation. That comes only through the atonement of the Savior.

And so when my peace is unsettled, I know it is on my knees that I will find it again. Quietly he speaks, "You are my daughter. No matter what is going on around you, all you need to do is act in accordance with that truth." I find that truth in the scriptures, in the *Ensign*, in daily prayer, in keeping the commandments, in my association with his other daughters, and most of all, in attending the temple regularly. I find peace as these actions bring me once more to a remembrance of my Savior and his atoning sacrifice for me.

Katie Marie Hansen is a homemaker and the mother of six children. She has taught in Primary and served in the Scouting program and in Young Women.

"Where Can I Turn for Peace?"

VALERIE ANN DECORA GUIMARÃES

The times in which we live today can certainly be trying, especially if we are without the gospel and a firm testimony of Jesus Christ. As Latter-day Saint women, we need not fear the times ahead. We can take courage and hold on together as we labor in the Lord's vineyard in our homes, in our ward families, and in our communities. With the hymn "Where Can I Turn for Peace" as a reference, I will attempt to share the story of my quest for peace (*Hymns of The Church of Jesus Christ of Latter-day Saints* [Salt Lake City: The Church of Jesus Christ of Latter-day Saints, 1985], no. 129).

> *Where can I turn for peace?*
> *Where is my solace*
> *When other sources cease to make me whole?*

In these tumultuous times, we can know peace as the Savior has promised. In John 14:27 we read: "Peace I leave with you, my peace I give unto you: not as the world giveth, give I unto you. Let not your heart be troubled, neither let it be afraid."

The world would have us believe that peace comes from an external force, far removed from us. It seeks to appeal to our "natural [wo]man" desires and appetites (Mosiah 3:19). For example, each day businesses spend millions of dollars in advertisements, targeted directly and predominantly at women, to convince us that we need to improve our outward appearance or increase our material possessions to find happiness or peace. Indeed, changing

147

our looks, improving our social status, or obtaining an overabundance of material possessions might bring us a kind of happiness. Yet we know that this type of happiness leaves us yearning for something of greater permanence.

As a child, I lacked the strength of a family well-founded in gospel principles. Though some members of my family belonged to the Church, church activity was not deemed important. I, too, became inactive at the age of twelve and found myself seeking peace in the world. The peace the world gives is tied up in material possessions, worldly knowledge, and sensuous desires. These false representatives of happiness loom overhead like glimmering signs on a dark, uncertain road, serving only to draw one further and further along toward certain destruction.

In retrospect, I know that a wise and loving Heavenly Father helped me to see where that path would lead. In a dream, I found myself in a cold, thick mist of darkness. I began to feel my way through the darkness, trying to escape from it. The mist left, and though my surroundings were still dark, I knew that that is what spiritual death would feel like—I would cease to exist, as if I had never lived. I awoke suddenly with a very clear remembrance of that terrible feeling.

From that time forward I spent much time and effort trying to prepare my life to learn of Heavenly Father once again. Though I had long forgotten the Primary lessons I had received as a child, once I began to desire to return to activity, I could remember the feelings of love and warmth I had felt so strongly after my participation in Church activities. Those feelings beckoned me on toward Heavenly Father.

> *When with a wounded heart, anger, or malice,*
> *I draw myself apart,*
> *Searching my soul?*
>
> Hymns, no. 129

President Ezra Taft Benson said, "Be warned that some of the greatest battles you will face will be fought within the silent chambers of your own soul" (*Teachings of Ezra Taft Benson* [Salt

Lake City: Bookcraft, 1988], 400–401). My quest for peace and happiness seemed almost too easy at first. I naïvely thought that my newfound desire to return to the Church would erase the painful past. The piercing remembrance of physical and sexual abuse, poverty, and the sins of commission overshadowed the strides that my family and I were making in drawing nearer to the Savior.

I had a daughter from a previous marriage whom I loved very much, and I yearned to have a child with my new husband. By the fourth month of my pregnancy, I realized that it was not to be. It was an ectopic pregnancy, and after surgery I learned the painful news that I could not give birth to any more children. My heart ached, and my faith wavered. I reasoned that this should not have happened to me because I was no longer "persecuting the church" (Philippians 3:6) and was striving to be obedient to Heavenly Father's commandments. I felt I was being punished for my wrongdoing, as any adult who had suffered physical and sexual abuse as a child might be prone to think. I became depressed and angry, and I fell into the depths of despair. My daughter was a busy teen, and my husband was a busy medical student. Though they knew of my pain and loved me very much, they were incapable of giving me what I needed most: peace to my soul.

Happier times came as my husband took the discussions and joined the Church. I attended the temple for my own endowments, and soon afterward my husband and I were sealed in the Salt Lake Temple. We moved to a new city, eager to begin our new careers and serve in our new ward. Then, without warning, my teenaged daughter announced that she would be moving to live with her biological father. It seemed that our newfound love of the gospel and of the Savior were stifling to her. I was alone. My husband was busy with his internal medicine residency, and my daughter was miles away. My faith wavered, and I found myself on bended knee, pleading with my Father in Heaven to let this bitter cup pass me by.

Though I was weak, full of pride, and faithless, a merciful Heavenly Father helped me to see the error of my thinking. In a dream I saw myself kneeling at the feet of a man. His feet were in sandals tied up around his ankles below his robe. I slowly began to recognize who he was. I began to cry. The tears flowed freely, and they bathed his feet. I could not look upon his face, feeling my shame, and I knelt even lower. I wiped his feet with my hair, and when I finished he held my hand and helped me to my feet.

I realized that in my depths of despair, I had been unable to forgive myself of my weaknesses and past sins. It was evident that the Savior remembered them no more, but I had clung to them as a heavy weight, thus slowing my progression. A tremendous burden was lifted from me! How true the scriptures ring as we read in Matthew 11:28–30: "Come unto me, all ye that labour and are heavy laden, and I will give you rest. Take my yoke upon you, and learn of me; for I am meek and lowly in heart: and ye shall find rest unto your souls. For my yoke is easy, and my burden is light."

The Savior is the balm we need to heal our wounded hearts, to calm our fears, and to speak peace to our souls. His infinite atonement provides healing balm liberally to all those who seek him and learn of him. President Howard W. Hunter said, "We must know Christ better than we know him; we must remember him more often than we remember him; we must serve him more valiantly than we serve him" (*Ensign*, May 1994, 64). In Doctrine and Covenants 19:23 we read: "Learn of me, and listen to my words; walk in the meekness of my Spirit, and you shall have peace in me."

Where can I turn for peace?

At times when our lives seem to be in order and we are striving to live as Heavenly Father wants us to live, adversity may strike. We may expect adversity to enter our lives when we are living unworthily. Yet the adversity that tests our faith in God when we are striving to live worthily seems to be the hardest of all.

In the spring of 1994, my daughter was diagnosed with a serious mental illness. My heart ached as she struggled from day to day. I humbly petitioned the Lord to help this beautiful young woman to become well. A peace beyond description filled my bosom after I concluded my prayer. Heavenly Father let me know in no uncertain terms that he was in charge. He was watching over her and would be merciful unto her. In the fall she returned to school, and within a few months, she was stabilized and enjoying her young life.

In February of 1996, my daughter began to experience what we thought were side effects from her medications; however, an MRI (magnetic resonance imaging) revealed a microadenoma in her pituitary gland. I pondered her plight. Why? Hasn't she suffered enough? As I thought upon these questions in sacrament meeting one Sunday, we began to sing the sacrament hymn, "Upon the Cross of Calvary":

> Upon the cross of Calvary
> They crucified our Lord
> And sealed with blood the sacrifice
> That sanctified his word.
>
> Upon the cross he meekly died
> For all mankind to see
> That death unlocks the passageway
> Into eternity.
>
> Upon the cross our Savior died,
> But, dying, brought new birth
> Through resurrection's miracle
> To all the sons of earth.

Hymns, no. 184

Tears flowed as I struggled to sing the hymn. The Savior had suffered for my sins. He gladly bore my stripes, and though I did not want to see my daughter suffer, didn't Heavenly Father also anguish in the suffering of his Only Begotten Son? Could I ask for less? Peace filled my soul again, as it was made manifest to me that all would be well.

I testify that amidst sore trials, amidst troubled times in our society, we as Latter-day Saint women can know peace. We need not fear the times ahead. We can take courage and hold on together as we labor in the Lord's vineyard in preparation for his second coming. As daughters of God, we can be as beacons in the night to women who lack the gospel in their lives. As sisters in Zion, we can strengthen and uplift one another in times of need. The balm we borrow from the Lord can assure that there will be balm of Gilead in our homes and in our communities.

Valerie Ann DeCora Guimãraes is a registered nurse. She and her husband, Paulo R. S. Guimãraes are the parents and foster parents of two children. She serves as a youth Sunday School teacher and an early-morning seminary teacher.

Index